100 DAYS OF WISDOM FROM THE WORLD'S WISEST KING

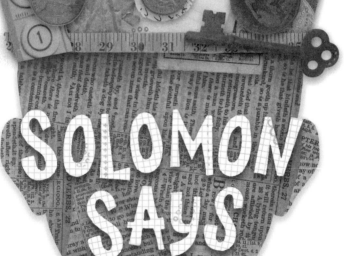

SOLOMON SAYS
Devotional

Sarah Humphrey and Amy Parker

ART BY HOLLI CONGER

B&H
kids
Nashville TN

To my tweens: Ella, Lucy, and Oliver. You are the treasures of my heart.
Your honest wisdom has brought me life. I love being your mom.—SH

I dedicate this book to my sons, as Solomon did,
praying they each live a life of Godly wisdom.—AP

Text copyright © 2021 by Amy Parker and Sarah Humphrey
Illustrations copyright © 2021 by B&H Publishing Group
Art by Holli Conger
All rights reserved.
Printed in the United States of America

978-1-0877-3463-7

Published by B&H Publishing Group,
Nashville, Tennessee.

Dewey Decimal Classification: J242.5
Subject Heading: DEVOTIONAL LITERATURE / SOLOMON, KING OF ISRAEL / CHRISTIAN LIFE

1 2 3 4 5 6 • 25 24 23 22 21

DEVOTIONS

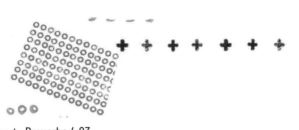

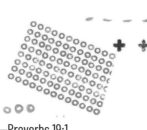

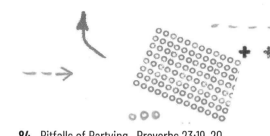

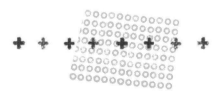

WHY PROVERBS?

I will give you a wise and discerning heart, so that there will never have been anyone like you, nor will there ever be.
—1 Kings 3:12 NIV

READ: 1 KINGS 3:4–15

Why in the world would anyone want to spend their time reading an ancient book of wisdom, of proverbs? What could some guy who lived thousands of years ago possibly have to say about *your* life, right *now*?

You'd be surprised.

First of all, much of the book of Proverbs wasn't written by just *any* guy—it was written by King Solomon. When Solomon became king (971 BC), he could have asked God for anything—riches, cool hair, his enemies to be flattened—but he didn't. He asked for the wisdom he would need to lead God's people. Because of that selfless request, God made Solomon "greater in riches and wisdom than all the other kings of the earth" (2 Chronicles 9:22 NIV). To put it in dollars, Solomon's yearly gold income *alone* was 666 talents (1 Kings 10:14-15), around $1 billion in today's dollars. Add to that his livestock, gifts from other rulers, income from traders, and you've got a pretty astronomical amount of wealth. God certainly gave Solomon what he asked for—and so much more.

Solomon, the richest, wisest man in the world, knew the power of wisdom. He knew it because he lived it. And now he's sharing it with us. Doesn't that sound like something worth exploring?

So let's dig in to this book of wisdom, this collection of proverbs. Let's see what that ancient King Solomon has to say—because this kind of wisdom can change a mind, change a heart, change *the world*.

Let's pray that it does just that.

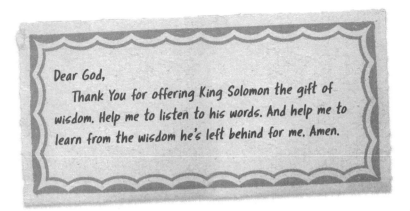

Dear God,
Thank You for offering King Solomon the gift of wisdom. Help me to listen to his words. And help me to learn from the wisdom he's left behind for me. Amen.

King/Queen _____ (your name here!)

So, let's say you're now the king or queen, and you want to pass on your legacy of wisdom to someone else. What would your letter say? What would your proverbs be?

_____

_____

_____

_____

_____

_____

_____

_____

_____

_____

_____

_____

THE BEGINNING

The fear of the LORD is the beginning of knowledge, but fools despise wisdom and instruction.—Proverbs 1:7 NIV

READ: PROVERBS 1:1–7

As wise as Solomon was, he knew real wisdom came from somewhere besides himself. It comes from God! God is the smartest, wisest, and wealthiest of anyone, anywhere. Everything in the world is His! (See Psalm 50:12.) Solomon got a glimpse of God's knowledge by doing one thing: asking for it in prayer. Can you imagine? He got the instructions for a good life simply by talking to God about it! From those conversations in prayer, Solomon knew that we'd have two choices: to live wisely or to live foolishly. And those two choices will give us very different results.

If you could read the recipe for a life of goodness, wouldn't you want to? That's what Solomon gives us in Proverbs! Who *doesn't* want to be wiser and get some instructions for life? Treat people in a way that is right and just and fair? Have guidance and understanding throughout life? I'm not seeing a downside to reading what he's sharing with us. You?

So, here is our first step: the beginning of the beginning. "The fear of the LORD is the beginning of knowledge." To gain real knowledge, that eternal truth to guide you for a lifetime, it has to begin with a fear, an awe, an interest in God and His ways, His truths.

Dear Lord,
I don't pretend to know Your thoughts or understand Your ways. But I'll start right here. I'll start with You. You are awesome and powerful, and the universe is Yours. I will never fully understand all that You are, but help me to begin with a fear and a reverence for You. Amen.

One of the best ways to understand "the fear of the Lord" is to open your eyes to the beauty of nature. It's God's majesty and creativity that show us just how big God is and just how small we are.

Go out, right now, and take in the awesomeness of the Lord. Stand under a starry sky. Feel the grass between your toes or the dirt in your palms. Marvel at the clouds bringing the rain. Wherever you are, whatever you're doing, take a moment to feel Him all around you and to be in awe of all He has made. When you're finished, save a little piece of that awesomeness here. Press a leaf between these pages. Write a song. Sketch a tree. Press your dirt-covered handprint into the paper. And always remember that this fear, this awe, is the beginning of knowing God and all that He is.

SOLOMON SAYS: *Go to page 98 for more about fear.*

PARENTAL UNITS

Hear the instruction of your father, and do not forsake the teaching of your mother.—Proverbs 1:8 MEV

READ: PROVERBS 1:8-9

Although "the fear of the LORD is the beginning of knowledge" (Proverbs 1:7), listening to our parents is not far behind. Sometimes that's easier said than done, huh?

Sometimes it's easy to think parents just don't get it, that they don't understand your life or feelings. But here's the thing, they likely do! It's hard to imagine, but they were also your age once and have experienced what that feels like. They can remember what it was like to be a kid, and they also know what it's like to be an adult.

I can tell you this without a doubt: you have parents or teachers or adult leaders in your life who love you so very much. And even though they aren't perfect (who is?), they are truly trying to give you all the skills and guidance and gifts that you'll need to be a good and Godly human. This is why God gave us those parents and teachers and leaders—and also why He reminds us again and again in His Word that we need to listen to them. He knew we'd need the reminder!

✢ ✢ ✢ ✢ ✢ ✢ ✢

Dear Lord,

You know my heart and my feelings, and You know the heart and feelings of my parents and the other adults who love me. Please help me to listen well, to think through decisions carefully, and to respect my parents' advice along the way. Thank You for giving me the caring adults I would need here on earth. Amen.

Ask one of your parents to hang out for some one-on-one time. It can be as simple as sitting on the front porch or going out to dinner to talk. Ask them about life when they were a kid—maybe what music they listened to, what they loved to do, what they wish they'd done differently. You may be surprised at what you learn! Use the space below to jot down some questions and write down their answers.

1
2
3
4
5
6
7
8
9
10
11
12
13
14
15
16
17
18
19
20
21

FIRE ALARMS

If sinful men entice you, do not give in to them.
—Proverbs 1:10 NIV

READ: PROVERBS 1:10-19

Have you ever had a set of friends that made an alarm go off in your brain? Like, you weren't sure whether you could trust him or her, or not? It takes wisdom to decide whether a friendship is a good connection.

If a friend ever wants you to do something that you don't feel comfortable with, Solomon says it's a good idea not to "give in to them." Instead, it's best to pause, pray, and then do what you know is right! Taking a moment to train your brain for good decisions can save you a lot of trouble in the long run.

Solomon understood that sometimes relationships are tricky, and saying no to friends can feel very uncomfortable. You might not know whether they will get mad at you or possibly make fun of you. But you can remember: God is always with you through every tough situation. We can always trust God's Word, but we can't always trust our friends' words. It takes courage to admit that, but when we do, God will help us know when to say no to our friends.

Dear Lord,
Friendships can be complicated, and I need Your help to be in good relationships. Please give me the wisdom I need to make good friends, stand up for what's right in hard situations, and be an example of You even when it's hard. Amen.

Take a minute to think about the friendships in your life. Are most of your friends from your neighborhood, church, or school? Who are the friends who make good choices often? Who are the friends you might be unsure of, depending on their behavior or choices?

Draw a circle in the space below. Write your name inside the circle. Take three colors and write the names of several friends along the outside of the circle. Use green for the names of friends you know you can trust, use blue for friends who might struggle to be a good influence, and use red for friends who may not be the best choice at this time. Think this through, and use wisdom to decide which friendships you'd like to grow. Being kind to everyone is always the right decision, but choosing which friends you want to grow with is using wisdom!

PSST...LISTEN!

Whoever listens to me will live in safety and be at ease, without fear of harm.—Proverbs 1:33 NIV

READ: PROVERBS 1:20-33

Have you ever thought about all the voices you listen to each day? Voices of friends. Voices in video games or online. Voices of parents and teachers. We have so many voices speaking into our lives, each and every day. How do we know whom we're supposed to listen to?

What about the voice of God? Most of us don't typically hear a booming voice from heaven, but God still speaks. Most often, He speaks through His Word. He speaks through parents and pastors. Romans 1:20 says that His power and nature is revealed to us through creation. And He's speaking to you right now, through His Word printed at the top of this page.

God may not be the first one we think of when we need help or advice, but He is always right there, listening to you and ready to answer. If you have a Bible at home, you can open it and hear His voice anytime. If you need wisdom or guidance—you guessed it—you can go to Him in prayer. And when you're listening for His voice, when you're trusting Him to answer, you'll be surprised at how He shows up and speaks to you, sometimes just as clearly as the voice of a friend.

Once we realize that the voice of God is wise and real and true, we're ready for the wisdom of Proverbs 1:33. Listen. When we listen to the voice of God, what does He promise? "Safety." "Ease." "Without fear of harm." Of all the voices we listen to, let's listen to the one clear voice, the voice of truth, the voice of the One who created us and who promises to keep us safe, without fear of harm, through it all.

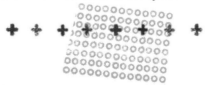

Dear Lord,

I know You're there, listening to me. Please help me always to remember that and to be willing to listen to Your voice. Help me not just to listen when You speak, but to seek Your voice first. Thank You for always being there, ready to listen and willing to speak. Amen.

Think about all of the voices mentioned earlier. Are there any that don't agree with what God says to you? Write down some of the negative or untrue things you've heard. Then search through your Bible (maybe with the help of a parent or pastor) to find out what God says instead. Cross out the things that are untrue, and write beside them what the voice of truth says to you.

_____

_____

_____

_____

_____

_____

_____

SOLOMON SAYS: *Go to pages 44, 60, and 114 for more on wise listening!*

SEEK WISDOM

If you call out to insight and lift your voice to understanding, if you seek it like silver and search for it like hidden treasure, then you will understand the fear of the LORD and discover the knowledge of God. —Proverbs 2:3-5

READ: PROVERBS 2:1-5

A lot of things in this world are questionable. For example, what were people thinking in the eighties with all that hairspray? Yikes, right? In time, we can realize that what is popular now might not always stay that way. That's why it's good to know what God says is long-lasting, wise, and true. Because unlike popular trends, His ways never go out of style!

Just like clothes and hairstyles, the news and social media can also be worth questioning. Sometimes the world's answers to our problems aren't the best answers. Sometimes what the world says we should listen to doesn't line up with the Bible, simply because a lot of people don't know much about the Bible or believe it.

Proverbs 2:3 says to "call out to insight and lift your voice to understanding." In other words, if you have questions about what is right, true, or safe, it's always best to pray. When we ask God questions in our prayers and seek out answers in the Bible, He will hear and answer us!

Dear Lord,
    Thank You for having the right answers to every question I have! Help me to remember to go to You in prayer and seek truth in Your Word when I need an answer. I ask for Your wisdom, especially in a busy world with unclear answers. Amen.

IMPORTANT QUESTIONS

Have questions? Sometimes life can be busy, and it can be hard to find the right time to ask trusted adults all the questions you have. Take some time today to make an "Important Questions" envelope. Inside, write down any questions you have about situations in your life or events in the world. Pray about each one, then put the questions in the envelope and plan a Q&A time with Mom or Dad or a teacher to answer your questions. You can add to your envelope whenever you like and work on finding Bible verses to match them! Bonus: if you write down the answers to these questions, you'll have your own collection of wisdom, just like Solomon!

UPRIGHT POSITION

For the LORD gives wisdom. . . . He stores up sound wisdom for the upright; He is a shield for those who walk in integrity.—Proverbs 2:6–7 NASB

READ: PROVERBS 2:6-9

Proverbs 2:6 makes me think of the airplane announcement to "return your seats to an upright position." It's not often that we use that word, *upright*. And when we do, it's probably not in the way the Bible is using it here. What about "integrity"? You probably have an idea about what that means, but could you put it to work in your own life? The big question is: how can we shape our lives to where these verses are talking about *us*?

Think of someone you really trust. Someone who always tells the truth. Someone who is always trying to make the right decisions. Someone who tries to do the best for everyone involved. Do you have a person in mind? It's probably safe to say that this person is "upright," a person of "integrity." (And it's also someone you could go to if you're struggling with the concept.)

What could you learn from this person's life? What does she do that you do? What does he do that you don't?

If you live your life in a way that makes you proud, you can stand upright. If you are honest with your words and in your actions, if you treat others fairly, you can earn the badge of integrity. More than that, a life of integrity is one that God responds to—by offering sound wisdom and a shield of His mighty power. And *that's* just two verses of the Bible. Throughout our trip through Proverbs, throughout your life, you'll see that a life of integrity is a life God rewards.

Dear God,

Thank You for Your examples of integrity. Help me to look to those examples when I need guidance, when I'm faced with tough decisions, and when nobody's looking. Help me to choose integrity even when it's hard. Amen.

The Secret to Success

Get a piece of paper, or even cardboard, and create a little plaque. Write on this plaque the most important piece of wisdom that you've learned so far. Now take that little plaque and give it away to someone. Give away wisdom, just as the Lord gives to you.

SOLOMON SAYS: *Go to page 86 for more rewards of righteousness.*

HAPPY OBEDIENCE

For wisdom will enter your heart, and knowledge will delight you. Discretion will watch over you, and understanding will guard you.—Proverbs 2:10-11

- - - - → **READ: PROVERBS 2:10-22**

Have you ever noticed when you work hard or make a good decision that you feel really good on the inside? God created us so that we have pleasure when we do what is right! Isn't that awesome? Solomon gives us all kinds of reminders about how wisdom will delight us. Even when a situation or decision is hard, we will feel happy from the inside out when we know we've been obedient.

It might seem like a strange question, but what are some of your favorite ways to obey? Can you think of a few chores around your house that you like to do? Or can you think of a few of your parents' rules you always make sure to follow? How do you feel when you've done your best work or followed through on a decision you knew was right? On the flip side, how do you feel when you know you let laziness creep in or didn't follow through? Doing what is right always makes a difference, and it helps us grow in the understanding of how life works best. It's why Solomon says that understanding will guard us; one good decision leads to another good decision!

Dear God,
    Thank You for making us shine when we follow Your wisdom. Help me to make good choices and always seek to learn more about Your ways. Give me a deep confidence in knowing Your way is the best way. Amen.

Grab a few pieces of paper, a pencil, and some markers. Take a few minutes to write yourself an encouraging note about your journey with wisdom. It can say anything from "Good job!" to "Keep it up!" or "God is with you!" You can make it more detailed and include specific choices that you're proud of.

You may also want to make a few notes about a time when you did not make a good decision. What happened then? We know that even in our mistakes, God is faithful to us as we learn how to repent, ask Him to help us make a better choice, and then follow through the next time. You might also want to write a note to remind yourself: "God is faithful!"

Decorate your sign however you like, put it in an envelope, and address it to yourself. Then ask your mom or dad to mail it to you when they think you need that encouragement. It will be a nice surprise for all the work you're putting into learning wisdom. Solomon says, "You are doing awesome in your wisdom journey!"

EAT YOUR PEAS

Don't forget my teaching, but let your heart keep my commands; for they will bring you many days, a full life, and well-being.—Proverbs 3:1–2

READ: DEUTERONOMY 11:18

Raise your hand if you love peas. Anyone? Maybe you eat them just because your mom tells you to. (Raising hand.) And your mom probably also reminds you that those tiny little peas (and other vegetables) eaten consistently can make a big difference in how healthy you feel.

Or consider LEGOs. A single, tiny brick isn't that impressive. But following the directions piece by piece by piece by piece gives you something pretty amazing in the end.

That's why part of King Solomon's wisdom is telling us *not to forget* the wisdom, "to keep" these commands. Or look at the more practical advice in Deuteronomy 11:18. It tells you to actually put signs on your hands and forehead so that you never forget God's teaching! The point is: *Do whatever it takes* to remember God's wisdom so that—piece by piece, little by little—you can keep His commands.

One little pea-sized decision may not make a big difference at the moment. But a lifetime of small decisions to keep God's commands? Well now, that will build you a pretty amazing life!

Dear God,
   I know that You're building something amazing in my life. Please help me to remember that and to make small, wise decisions every single day to help build me up according to Your plans. Help me find a way to keep Your wisdom in my heart. Thank You for Your all-knowing wisdom. Amen.

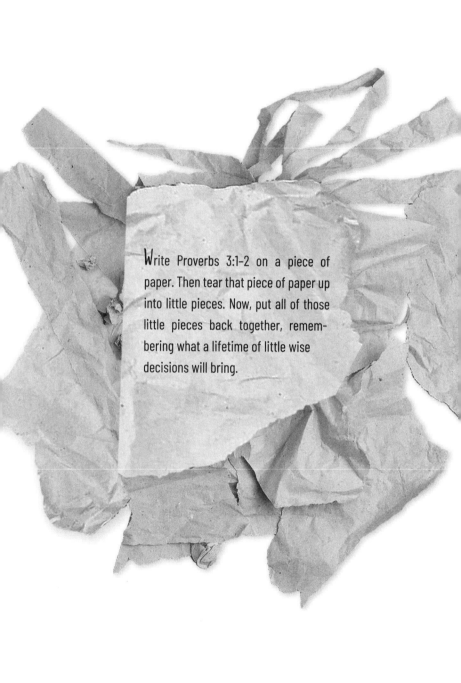

Write Proverbs 3:1-2 on a piece of paper. Then tear that piece of paper up into little pieces. Now, put all of those little pieces back together, remembering what a lifetime of little wise decisions will bring.

LIVE LOYAL!

Never let loyalty and faithfulness leave you . . . write them on the tablet of your heart.—Proverbs 3:3

READ: PROVERBS 3:3-4

Have you ever heard the phrase: "If you want a friend, be a friend"? It simply means that when you are loyal and faithful as a friend, you will attract more friends who are loyal and faithful. Solomon is quick to remind us to write loyalty on our hearts.

But what does that mean? Getting out a marker and writing on our chests? Hmm. Probably not. Sticking to your word, following through on what you say you'll do, and being the kind of person you want in a friend are great ways to show loyalty. These choices will keep your friendships healthy and happy!

Doesn't it feel good to have people in your life who you know will be faithful to you even if you go through a hard time or make mistakes? That's what loyalty and grace look like—loving one another despite our failures! It is wise to extend grace and mercy to others because we will need grace and mercy at times in our lives too. Being able to stay true to grace, mercy, and forgiveness with others is an important part of faithful and loyal friendship.

Dear God,
   Thank You for the people in my life who are faithful and loyal to me. Please help me to be a faithful and loyal friend. Please give me the grace to pay attention to those around me and to remember to bless them with my friendship. Amen.

Think of three of your best friends. Write their names below and maybe add a few things you like about them. Now think of some things they may be struggling with. Maybe you have a friend whose parents are divorcing. Or perhaps a friend is struggling with a subject in school, and he or she is nervous about getting a bad report card. Do you have any friends who are sick? Maybe you know someone who has had a family member pass away recently. Spend a few minutes thanking God for each one of those friends by name. Say a prayer for each friend and each situation, and ask God to bless them with His goodness and love. Being a good friend is always a good way to live loyal!

GOD'S TWO FEET

Trust in the LORD with all your heart, and do not rely on your own understanding.—Proverbs 3:5

READ: PROVERBS 3:5-8

Proverbs 3:5 is probably a verse you've heard before, maybe even memorized. And it's a good one to know. But it's a tough one to practice.

After all, how many times have you been told to be self-sufficient? To stand on your own two feet? But your own two feet are only as strong as *your own* two feet. Imagine, however, if we stood on the infinite knowledge and power of God. Wouldn't that change things a bit?

If you read further down in Proverbs 3:8, you'll see the result of trusting God instead of yourself: "healing for your body and strengthening for your bones." Isn't that funny? Isn't that exactly how God works? When you exchange your own wisdom for God's, when you trust in Him instead of yourself, He strengthens your body and your bones so that, through Him, you *can* stand on your own two feet—because your own two feet are standing on the wisdom of God.

Whatever questions you have today, whatever tough decisions you're facing, just know that you don't have to face them on your own. Have you made a mistake and you don't know what to do next? Are you worried about a friend or family member? You don't have to have all the wisdom and power within yourself to answer all the questions and make all the decisions.

Go to God, seek His wisdom—through prayer, through Godly parents, or through His Word. When you do, you'll face the uncertainty of this world with the wisdom of the One who made it. And that, my friend, is all the wisdom you'll ever need.

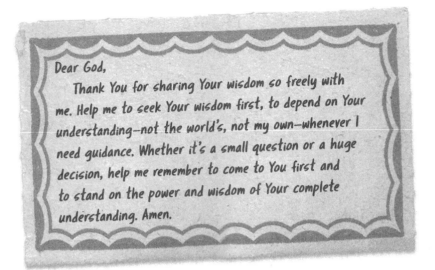

Dear God,

Thank You for sharing Your wisdom so freely with me. Help me to seek Your wisdom first, to depend on Your understanding—not the world's, not my own—whenever I need guidance. Whether it's a small question or a huge decision, help me remember to come to You first and to stand on the power and wisdom of Your complete understanding. Amen.

Grab a rock, a tissue, and a Bible.

First, slightly wet the tissue. Now, have someone gently hold it out flat while you set the rock on it. What happens?

Now place the rock on your Bible. What happens?

Compared to God's understanding, our understanding is about as strong as a wet tissue. It just won't stand up to the weight of this world. But God's wisdom, His Word, and His understanding are *always* a strong foundation to stand on!

FULL BARNS

Honor the LORD with your possessions and with the first produce of your entire harvest; then your barns will be completely filled, and your vats will overflow with new wine.
—Proverbs 3:9-10

READ: MATTHEW 6:33-34

In Matthew 6:33, Jesus shares these wise words: "Seek first the kingdom of God and his righteousness, and all these things will be provided for you." It's safe to say that Solomon is sharing much of this same wisdom in Proverbs 3, and both verses encourage us to honor God with everything we own. Our barns (or our lives) will be filled as a result of our obedience. Isn't that something you've heard before?

This verse does have a good point—even if you don't live on a farm! It states that when you give thanks to God and follow His ways first, He will always provide what you need in return—and then some! So maybe that's not filling your barn with cows or grain (or maybe it is!), but no matter what you need, God promises to make sure you have more than enough.

Isn't it interesting that the God who gives you such good gifts also wants you to learn how to give your gifts back to Him? When you are responsible with what God gives you, it makes it easy for Him to provide you with all the other things you need such as Godly friends, courage, and wisdom. Giving back to God in prayer and through your earnings are simple ways for you to show God you believe in Him fully, trust His instructions, and are grateful for the opportunities He gives you. I bet your barn will be overflowin'!

Dear God,

Thank You for the simple instructions to serve You first. As I remember to love You and then love the people around me, please bless me with the joy of knowing You more. Help me to see You first in everything I do so that my life will overflow with Your abundance. Amen.

Have you ever heard of *firstfruits*? It's a term used in the Bible that reminds us to give God the first part of our earnings (or crops) to show our love for Him. Christians give their firstfruits or offering as a way to honor the Lord and help His work be done here on earth.

Have you ever thought of sharing what you've earned with God (or with your church)? If so, great job! If not, take this week to ask your mom or dad if you might be able to do a few extra chores around the house to earn a little bit of money. Thank God in prayer for the opportunity and ability to work hard, and then ask your parents to help you set aside the first chunk of the money to put in the offering basket next Sunday.

Giving back to your church with your time and money is a wonderful way to worship God. Keep your eyes open for how He will give you more responsibility! He loves watching you obey His Word.

CORRECTiON!

Do not despise the LORD's instruction, my son, and do not loathe his discipline; for the LORD disciplines the one he loves, just as a father disciplines the son in whom he delights.—Proverbs 3:11-12

READ: 2 SAMUEL 7:12-16

I love it when I'm corrected . . . when I'm told to do *this* not *that* . . . when I get red marks on my tests . . . when I get privileges taken away . . . when I am sent to my room. Don't you?

No. No, we absolutely do not. And yet, Solomon has the nerve to tell us *not to* despise, dislike, or "loathe" the Lord's instruction and discipline. Why?

Okay, "instruction" is an easy one. We understand that sometimes we have to follow steps one, two, and three to get a certain result. There's no way around it.

But discipline? It's painful! It can be embarrassing and discouraging. Still, if you touch a hot stove, you probably won't ever do it again. And that's a good thing, right? The temporary pain is bad, but never again sizzling your fingers on a stove? That's definitely a good thing.

When you read the passage from 2 Samuel listed above, you'll find something that may help even more. Do you see it? Four words: "when he does wrong" (2 Samuel 7:14). Not "if," not "maybe," not "worst-case scenario," but "when." God is talking about *Solomon* here, the son of King David, the very same Solomon who God already knew would be the world's wisest king. And God said, "When he does wrong . . ."

God already knows that even the wisest of us are going to mess up. The difference is not in the mistakes we make, but in how we respond when we make them. When you feel God saying, "Please don't ever do that, ever, ever again," you're feeling His love, you're feeling His instruction, and you're feeling His grace to get it right the next time. That's definitely a discipline we can learn to appreciate.

Dear God,

Thank You for Your grace. Thank You for knowing I'm going to mess up and for sending Jesus as the sacrifice for when I do. Help me to look and listen for Your instruction—and to follow it. And help me learn to appreciate Your discipline. Help me to remember that it is simply Your love, guiding me back to the right path. Thank You for leading the way. Amen.

Get a coin or other small, shiny object and hide it somewhere in your house or yard. Now, ask a family member to find it, using only your direction and correction. When they're going the right way, say, "Warmer." When they're going the wrong way, say, "Colder." Keep going until they have found the treasure.

Would they have found the coin without your direction and correction? Probably not anytime soon. When we follow God's instructions and respond correctly to His discipline, we are well on our way to finding the treasures He has waiting for us.

ORGANIZING THE WORLD

The LORD founded the earth by wisdom and established the heavens by understanding. By his knowledge the watery depths broke open, and the clouds dripped with dew.
—Proverbs 3:19-20

READ: PROVERBS 3:13-20

Can you imagine God creating the earth? I'm sure you've heard the story in Genesis before. Our Creator made the world in just six days and took one extra day to rest. In the middle of forming the sun and moon, birds and fish, people and more, God was already using His creative wisdom as our foundation. Way before Solomon said anything, God was getting started with what was most important. (Of course He was!)

Today's verses in Proverbs tell us that God's genius made the depths break open and the clouds drip with dew. Doesn't that sound beautiful? It seems that not only does God enjoy simple brilliance in creation, but His knowledge also reflects peace and order. It just goes to show us that God planned everything He brought into existence, and He made sure to put it all in its perfect place. His Word shows us how we can know Him and His ways. His creativity also brings us deep peace, so we can remember that everything good in the world started with Him.

Remembering God's power, presence, and order gives us confidence that He will always be there for us, and He will always give us wisdom when we ask for it. It all started with Him in the first place!

Dear Lord,

Thank You for Your constant creativity, beauty, and peace in this world You've created. You are wonderful! We give You praise for everything Your hands have made. You are true, good, faithful, and beautiful. Amen.

Look around your bedroom and see if there is anything that needs to be thrown away or cleared out. Make sure that your bed is made, your clothes are folded, and your stuff is clean and organized.

After you have spent time getting your room clean and pulled together, take a moment to think about how life can be peaceful when things are clean and orderly. Then get out some art supplies. Create a piece of art that reminds you of the peace that God brings to your heart. It can be a picture of giant waves, or clouds dripping with dew, or anything else that shows the beauty of God in your life! Place your new art in your organized room, and enjoy.

CONFIDENCE

The LORD will be your confidence and will keep your foot from a snare.—Proverbs 3:26

READ: PROVERBS 3:21-26

What gives you confidence? What do you do well? Are you a fast runner? Can you sink free throws nonstop? Can you draw or write or sing? These are all wonderful gifts, but we have to be careful to put our confidence in the Giver of those gifts and not the gifts themselves.

We don't know exactly when Solomon wrote this part of Proverbs, but it sounds like by the time he did, he had lived some life and maybe even made a few bad decisions. In verse 21, he warns, "Maintain your competence [your abilities] and discretion [good judgment]. My son, don't lose sight of them" (HCSB). Doesn't that sound like someone who *had* lost sight of them?

Sadly, we do know that later in Solomon's life, he drifted away from God. He went against the wisdom of this verse and placed his focus and his confidence in things other than God, things that were wrong, things that would not last. And through his own life, he showed us the results: his God-given gifts of wisdom and abundance withered away. He left behind a splintered kingdom and a son who proved to be a foolish ruler (1 Kings 12, 14). Solomon himself showed us how the greatest wisdom is worthless if we choose to ignore it.

We can fill our lives with lots of wonderful things. We can excel and delight in our accomplishments. But as Solomon learned, we must keep our focus and our confidence on the all-knowing, all-powerful, everlasting God who created us to be our best through Him.

FOCUS!

Dear God,

Thank You for my amazing gifts. Thank You for knowing exactly what I would need in this life and always helping me to use those gifts to bring You glory. When I get a little too confident in myself or in the things of this world, please remind me that they are all so small compared to the power and glory I find in You. Thank You for caring enough to let me share in those gifts and that glory. Amen.

What gifts has God given you? Maybe you draw or sing or build things. Spend a little time planning a way to exhibit those gifts. Have a concert. Set up an art gallery in the hallway. Plan out your next project to build. Confidently share your gifts with your family and friends, and then praise God for giving you fast feet or a beautiful voice or strong hands. Give all the glory back to the God who gave you these wonderful gifts.

GIVE AWAY GOOD

When it is in your power, don't withhold good from the one whom it belongs. Don't say to your neighbor, "Go away! Come back later. I'll give it tomorrow"—when it is there with you.—Proverbs 3:27–28

READ: PROVERBS 3:27–30; JOHN 3:16

Generosity is one of God's greatest traits. He was so merciful that He gave us Jesus to die for our sins and to take our place for all our mistakes and failures. Not only did He send His Son to die for us, but He also encourages us to respond to His gift of love by giving away the good in our lives to others who need it. When we share our time, skills, and kindness with others, we are giving the way Jesus gave to us.

Sometimes it can seem hard to give away good because we might be tired or grumpy, or maybe we just don't feel like it at the time. It happens! We all have days when we might not feel like giving a good attitude or a good gift, but Proverbs reminds us not to hold back in giving good to people who deserve it. Waiting to be kind, loving, and generous would benefit no one. Choosing to give away good is like turning on a light in the dark! It reminds us to shine instead of grumble. It gives us joy instead of bitterness.

The next time you are tempted to hold back your kindness or your good works, remind yourself that wisdom tells you otherwise. You can be the bright light in someone's day by giving away what God has given you!

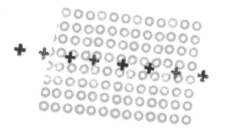

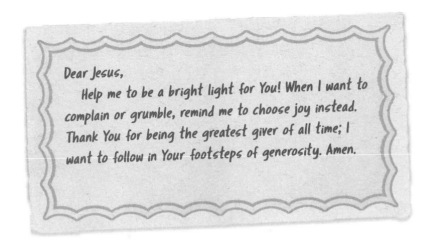

Dear Jesus,
   Help me to be a bright light for You! When I want to complain or grumble, remind me to choose joy instead. Thank You for being the greatest giver of all time; I want to follow in Your footsteps of generosity. Amen.

Make a list of three to five of your strongest character traits. Some examples could be *honest, hard worker, thoughtful,* or *kind.* Once you've made your list, think of different ways you can share those traits with other people around you. When you do this, you are giving away the goodness that God has planted in your heart and life! This generosity makes you a leader and helps you grow while also helping others grow.

You might also want to make a list of three to five character traits where you struggle a bit and could use some growth. Take the time to say a prayer, and ask God to help you change these traits. When you feel like sinking into a bad behavior, remind yourself of your prayer! Try to change your bad habit into a good one until it becomes part of you.

17

FIGHTERS AND FOOLS

Don't envy a violent man or choose any of his ways.
—Proverbs 3:31

READ: PROVERBS 3:32–35

Have you heard Aesop's fable about the sun and the wind? The sun and wind were arguing over who was stronger and decided to prove it by seeing which one could make a man take off his coat. The wind blew violently, trying to tear the coat off the man, but the man only pulled the coat tighter. When it was the sun's turn, the wise sun simply shined. And of course, in no time, that man was taking off his coat.

It's such a strong example of how our actions affect others and how violence and force are rarely (um, never?!) the best way to get things done. Solomon shared this wisdom with us long before Aesop did, and he goes on (in vv. 32–35) to tell us how God responds. (Spoiler alert: it's not good.)

But do you see the others included in this category of "fools"? The "devious," the "wicked," and "those who mock"? A "devious" person is always scheming, tricking others to get his own way. A "wicked" person is mean and hateful and up to no good. But the one that seems more innocent on the surface is "those who mock," those who make fun of others or things. Making fun of a teacher or a sister or someone's clothes (both out loud or even to yourself) can seem lighthearted enough, but in God's eyes, a person who mocks is also a "fool." An unkind word can be just as violent as trying to tear off a man's coat.

So from now on, whenever you're tempted to get your own way, to be mean, or to make fun of someone, remember instead to be like the sun . . . and simply *shine*.

Dear God,

Thank You for reminding me of the best way to treat others. Please forgive me for when I've been a fool, when I've been mean or hurtful to the people around me. Help me always remember to be kind and to shine for Your glory. Amen.

A fable is a story including animals or nature that teaches us a lesson. Do you think you could write your own fable? Sure you can! Go outside and stand in the sun. Listen to the birds sing. Watch the ants work. Then write or draw your own fable. When you're finished, share it with your family or friends.

THE VALUE OF WISDOM

I am teaching you the way of wisdom; I am guiding you on straight paths. When you walk, your steps will not be hindered; when you run, you will not stumble. Hold on to instruction; don't let go. Guard it, for it is your life.
—Proverbs 4:11-13

READ: PROVERBS 4:1-13

Have you ever tried to run in the woods without a clear path? It's really difficult! You spend most of your time pushing tree branches and weeds out of the way, trying to jump over rocks and not trip in the process. You might end up with scratches on your legs or get hit in the face with wild sticks; it's just not the smartest thing to try to do!

On the other hand, have you ever tried to run through the woods on a clear pathway that was designed for joggers? If so, you saw that the trees were cleared, the path was either paved or leveled off, and the branches, rocks, and sticks were all out of the way. It makes it much easier to move faster and enjoy yourself. There is less chance of getting an injury, and you can look ahead with ease.

These verses from Solomon show us just that. He tells us that Proverbs is all about being taught wisdom and being guided to a straight path instead of a clunky, messy, dangerous one! Instructions from the Bible are like the hand of God clearing the way to make a nice running path for us. Staying on God's path keeps us safe, and it makes our journey so much more valuable. We always grow instead of fall.

Dear Lord,
Thank You for making a clear path for us. Help me to read and memorize Your Word so that I can walk and run freely. Open my eyes to see Your straight path, and help me to trust You even when I'm not sure which direction to go. Amen.

Take some time to go on a nature walk. On the walk, look for a few smooth stones that you can bring home to paint! Take a few minutes to paint the rocks with fun colors, and write "Proverbs 4:11-13" on them. You might also want to paint encouraging words like *wisdom*, *listen*, *walk*, or *run* across them. Set the rocks somewhere in your room to remind you that the Bible always helps us run on a clear path! Its instructions for life guide us to move forward with clarity, ease, and strength.

A SHINING LIGHT

The path of the righteous is like the light of dawn, shining brighter and brighter until midday.—Proverbs 4:18

READ: PROVERBS 4:14-19

There are some beaches around the world where, when you walk along them at night, you can look back and see your footprints glowing. They're not just shining in the moonlight but actually glowing in the dark! This rare effect is caused by a bunch of tiny plankton that glow in the sand when you step on them. You can actually leave a glowing path behind you!

If you read the entire passage given above (vv. 14–19), you'll see that Solomon points out the striking contrast between the path of righteousness (doing what's right) and the path of the wicked. We can easily feel the dark, draining emptiness of one path and the glowing warmth of the other.

The struggle between light and darkness is nothing new, but the Bible tells us how the story ends. Jesus said simply, "I am the light of the world" (John 8:12). And later, in Revelation 19:12, Jesus' eyes are like a "fiery flame" as He rides through the earth on a white horse, extinguishing the darkness.

Because of Jesus, the light wins in the end. But in the meantime, we have to choose our paths. With every choice we make, every step we take, we have to determine whether our steps will stumble in the darkness or leave a beautiful, glowing path of light. When we choose to do what's right, we not only illuminate our own paths, but we also bring light to the darkness of those who have lost their way.

Shine brightly, friends, and let the light of Jesus shine through you.

Dear Jesus,

Thank You for being the light of the world. And thank You for lighting the path, showing us the way we are supposed to walk. Help me to make the right choices each and every day so that I will not only be able to see my own path clearly but also light the way for someone else. When I am in darkness, help me to see Your light. Amen.

Ask your parents if you can do a little demonstration when it gets dark at your house. Get a flashlight, and turn out all the lights. Without using the flashlight, try to make it—slowly, carefully—from the kitchen to your room in the dark. Now turn the flashlight on and try it. Was that easier? Now try the same path one more time with all the lights back on.

This experiment may seem silly, but it makes a clear point. The more light you add, the easier it is to find your way. When we follow Jesus, the Light of the world, we'll still have to walk the path, but it will be a whole lot easier to find our way.

LiFE AND HEALTH

My son, pay attention to my words; listen closely to my sayings. Don't lose sight of them; keep them within your heart. For they are life to those who find them, and health to one's whole body. —Proverbs 4:20–22

READ: ACTS 17:28

We've all heard that we need to eat our veggies, drink our water, and take our vitamins. Moms and dads around the world are always telling their kids to eat good food and to move their bodies every day. Healthy food and exercise keep us strong so that we can live full lives!

Who would have thought that wisdom could be healthy for your body too? Lo and behold, that is what Solomon is saying to us in today's verse! He gives us the important advice to "listen closely" to his sayings and "keep them within your heart." He goes on to express, "They are life to those who find them, and health to one's whole body."

Wow! What important instruction for us! We can actually be healthy in our bodies when we listen to wisdom and instruction. It's as if the very words we are studying in this book are actually guidelines and medicine for our minds and our human frame. It's easy to forget that our spiritual food can be just as important for staying healthy in our day-to-day lives.

This goes to show that God thinks of us through a bigger picture, all the way around, and even in all our nooks and crannies. He knows how He's created us inside and out, and He knows exactly what we need to thrive!

Dear Lord,

It can be easy to be lazy or sluggish. I admit it. Help me to remember that food and exercise are fuel for my day. I want to make wise choices so that my body is full of strength and my heart is full of Your Word. Amen.

Have you ever done a food diary? It's a list of every bit of food you eat all day. Every time you eat, you write it down so that you can track what you're actually putting into your body.

A food diary can be a good reminder to choose healthier options, and it can also be helpful to remind us to choose wisdom in other ways. When we eat good food, we tend to make better choices. When we make one good choice, we'll likely make another!

Start a food diary today! Put a Bible verse at the top to remind you to feed your mind and body with the Word, as well as with a good snack! See how you feel after doing this for a day or two. If you like it, keep going, and share the idea with a friend.

GUARD YOUR HEART

Guard your heart above all else, for it is the source of life.
—Proverbs 4:23

READ: PROVERBS 4:23–27

Technically, medically, the heart is a vital organ. It sits roughly in the center of your chest and pumps blood to the rest of your body. Through the blood, your heart provides the rest of the body with the oxygen and nutrients it needs to function.

Maybe for that reason, for centuries, the heart has also been recognized as the center of emotion, the storage facility for our feelings. It's where, figuratively, our most important feelings and thoughts and wishes are held.

Heartbreaks and heartaches are terms of emotion, of course, not medical terms. However, not so surprisingly, the medical field has now uncovered a real medical condition called "broken heart syndrome,"[*] where the heart is damaged temporarily by stress. We also know that long-term stress can damage that vital organ, your heart, and lead to serious heart conditions. So, maybe, our figurative, emotional "heart" and the actual vital organ are a lot more connected than we think.

In Proverbs 4:23, Solomon tells us to guard our heart. He knew that like the vital organ, our emotional heart affects the rest of our bodies. If our heart is unhealthy, our mind and body will be unhealthy too.

To guard your physical heart, you want to eat right, exercise, and keep stress under control. For your emotional heart, you also want to feed it with good stuff, like God's Word and prayer. Keep it active by being kind and loving to others. And protect it from harm by being careful about what you allow into your heart and mind.

Keep a close watch over your heart—both physically and emotionally—because, as Solomon so wisely says, "It is the source of life."

---

[*] https://www.mayoclinic.org/diseases-conditions/broken-heart-syndrome/symptoms-causes/syc-20354617#:~:text=Broken%20heart%20syndrome%20is%20a,cardiomyopathy%20or%20apical%20ballooning%20syndrome.

Dear God,

Thank You for my miraculous body, for my heart that supplies the rest of my body with what it needs to function. Help me to keep my heart and mind healthy by feeding it with Your Word and by protecting it from hurtful, harmful things. Help me to exercise my heart through kindness and love. And help my heart, the source of life, to be a healthy, loving reflection of You. Amen.

Read Proverbs 4:23-27. Draw an outline of the human body, including the different parts mentioned in the passage. Draw a line to the parts mentioned and label each with the instructions Solomon gives. Write them in your own words, if you'd like. Are there any other instructions you can think of? Add them to your drawing. Hang it up as a reminder of how to guard your heart.

FORBIDDEN VILLAINS

Though the lips of the forbidden woman drip honey and her words are smoother than oil, in the end she's as bitter as wormwood and as sharp as a double-edged sword.
—Proverbs 5:3-4

READ: PROVERBS 5:1-8

Have you ever heard the word *forbidden* before? You might have heard your mom or dad say it when they were saying something like "I forbid you to do that!" It can mean stop, absolutely do not, or simply put: "No, no, no!"

Forbid is a very strong word, and it's usually used when adults are very serious about something. Typically, it's something dangerous that they might be trying to protect you from.

In Proverbs 5:3-4, Solomon describes a woman he says is "forbidden" and gives clear instructions not to go near her. She says a ton of "sweet" things, but they are all really lies. She's simply using nice words to get what she wants, and she will do so to make people obey her. Underneath, she's actually very bitter and angry, and she is out to get those she tries to persuade. Yikes! Sounds like the villain in a story, if you ask me!

Maybe you don't know a "forbidden woman," but I bet you know a few things in your parents' rule book that you are forbidden to do, such as use bad language, be disrespectful, or watch certain shows without approval. Knowing what those rules are can help you keep your eyes and ears open for making healthy decisions. If you don't know what is forbidden, you might get tricked into doing it. Wisdom knows the difference between a good choice and a forbidden one; it can change the whole world!

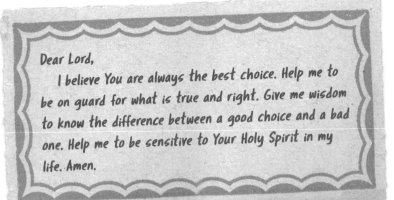

Dear Lord,
I believe You are always the best choice. Help me to be on guard for what is true and right. Give me wisdom to know the difference between a good choice and a bad one. Help me to be sensitive to Your Holy Spirit in my life. Amen.

This is a good day to have some one-on-one time with Mom or Dad or a grown-up who loves you! When you get a few minutes, talk about a few of the important rules they want you to always obey. Of course, there will be times when you make mistakes and mess up, but this time focus on the rules they always, always, always want you to follow. They probably have a few of them, and they probably can share the reasons why they do. (Ask them to spill their secrets as to why!)

Because they've lived more life than you, your parents have had a lot more opportunities to make good choices and also bad ones! This is a great time to find out why their advice is important.

23

SELF-CONTROL

You will say, "How I hated discipline, and how my heart despised correction. I didn't obey my teachers or listen closely to my instructors. I am on the verge of complete ruin before the entire community."—Proverbs 5:12-14

READ: GALATIANS 5:22-24

We've talked about how important correction and discipline are. We know a life that always rejects instruction doesn't end well. But did you know there's a little shortcut to avoiding correction and discipline?

It's nothing sneaky or tricky. In fact, it's a pretty mature skill that takes a lifetime to develop called *self-control*. I know, it sounds like another not-fun word like *discipline*. But wait till you see it in action.

Say you have a homework assignment due tomorrow. Do you (A) work on it? Or (B) play games and doodle for the next hour?

Let's start with option B. What do you think the result will be? I know because I have seen it countless times! The results are stressed-out parents, lots of nagging, zero family time, and a very tired you who still has homework to do.

What about option A? Ahh, it seems so simple. You go in your room, do your homework, and *voilà*! You have the rest of the night free! Everyone's happy!

So what does option A have that option B is missing? You guessed it! Self-control.

Self-control is just what it sounds like: being able to control *yourself*—instead of someone else doing it through discipline or correction. As simple as it sounds, it sure isn't easy. But when we believe in Jesus, we are helped by the Spirit. And as Galatians 5:22-24 tells us, one of the fruits (or benefits) of the Spirit is self-control.

Self-control takes a lot of practice and hard work. But stick to it and get a little help from the Spirit along the way. When you do, you'll see that life gets easier and happier for everyone.

Dear God,

I'm sorry for all the times I totally lack self-control. But I'd like to start working on that. Thank You for sending the Spirit to help me. Please help me to listen for that still, small voice that helps me stay on track. And thank You for loving me, even when I get a little out of control. Amen.

Think about some areas where you could use a little self-control. Maybe your parents are always telling you to turn off the TV or get off the computer or stay out of the snack drawer. Whatever it is, set a goal for yourself. Maybe it's "I'll only watch TV thirty minutes a day." Write down your goal, and underneath it, write M, T, W, Th, F for each day of the week. Put a star on each day when you have self-control. Put an X over each day when you missed the mark. Then, next week, try again, getting better and better every time you try. When it's feeling impossible, say a short prayer, and ask the Spirit for help!

SOLOMON SAYS: *To read more about the fruit of the Spirit, go to page 80.*

24

DON'T GET TANGLED

For a man's ways are before the LORD's eyes, and he considers all his paths. A wicked man's iniquities will trap him; he will become tangled in the ropes of his own sin.
—Proverbs 5:21–22

READ: PROVERBS 5:21–23; DEUTERONOMY 30:19

Have you ever heard the saying, "You've come to a fork in the road"? It doesn't mean a fork is actually in the road. It means the road splits into two paths. Imagine you are driving down one road for a long while when, all of a sudden, you now need to make a choice. You'll either turn left or turn right, one way or the other way. If you go one direction, it will lead you to a destination (hopefully it's the one you're looking for), and if you turn the other direction, it will take you, well, somewhere else.

Since we've been studying about wisdom, let's look deeper at the scenario Solomon explains in the verse above. He says that all the paths of our lives are marked out for us by God Himself, but we get to choose which way we are going to go. That's trusting of God to give us that responsibility.

If we aren't reading our Bibles or listening to the Godly adults in our lives, we might accidentally go down the path of wickedness and end up in a trap! Eek! We could get tangled up in our own sins and mistakes. But if we choose the path that God has laid out for us, with His Word leading the way, we will know that we can be free to get to the proper destination!

So the next time you come to a fork in the road, make sure you take a minute to remember what Solomon said—choose your path wisely!

Dear God,

Thank You for trusting me enough to make decisions in my life. Help me to remember to pray when I come to a fork in the road and need to make a choice. Remind me that You are always with me, and give me the eyes and ears to look for Your wisdom and love. Amen.

Got any plastic silverware in your house?

If so, grab a fork, and a permanent marker. (If not, perhaps you can pick some up the next time you're at the store.) You can also grab some glue and a few items to decorate your fork!

On the handle, write "Don't Get Tangled" and "Proverbs 5:21–23." Add some color and some tangled twine or string to your fork. Set it somewhere where you'll see it often so that you're consistently reminded to make wise choices, especially if things get complicated! There are "forks in the road" all the time throughout the day; your art will remind you to choose the path God has laid out for you!

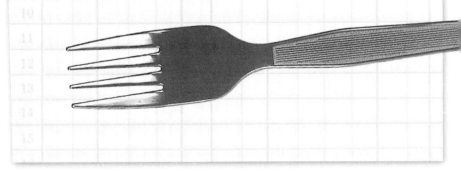

25

WATCH THE ANTS

Take a lesson from the ants, you lazybones. Learn from their ways and become wise!—Proverbs 6:6 NLT

READ: PROVERBS 6:6–11

If you could be any insect in the world, what would it be? A butterfly with big, beautiful wings? A beetle, with its tough outer shell? Or an ant, tiny but always hard at work?

Ants are fascinating creatures. You've probably heard it said that an ant can carry fifty (or even five thousand!) times its weight, which is amazing in itself. But did you know that ants have one of the longest life spans of any insect? They also hold the record for "the fastest movement in the animal kingdom," referring to how fast an ant can close its mouth.[*]

So when Solomon was giving advice to old "lazybones," it's no surprise that he instructed him to observe the ant. There's much to be learned from ants: how they all work together to build their homes and to provide food for the colony. But what Solomon points out is how they have no one to make them work, yet they still "labor hard all summer, gathering food for the winter" (v. 8).

What do you do when no one is looking? How hard do you work when no one is making you? How do you prepare for the season ahead? The tiny ant is hard at work, even when no one is looking. The ant keeps working not only for itself, but for its community, even though there's no boss to make him. And the ant works ahead, preparing for the season to come. In what way, every day, could you be more like the ant in the tasks you've been given?

Just think: if God packed that much wisdom into the behavior of a tiny ant, imagine how much more is waiting for us if we grow our own wisdom and put it to work.

---

[*] https://www.natgeokids.com/nz/discover/animals/insects/ant-facts/

Dear God,

Thank You for all the amazing wonder You've built into this world. And thank You for the example of the tiny ant. Help me to work hard without being told so that my home and my community will be a better place. Amen.

Go outside and look at all the amazing things God has created. See if you can find some ants and watch them work. Look around at the other creatures, and see what you can learn from them too. Listen for the bird that's always singing. Watch the squirrel burying food for another day. Keep an eye out for the caterpillar that will one day transform into a beautiful butterfly. Even the neighbor's dog, out for a walk, can teach us about enjoying each day. Spend some time in nature and, like Solomon, see what wisdom you can learn from the world God has created around you.

SEVEN THINGS

The LORD hates six things; in fact, seven are detestable to him: arrogant eyes, a lying tongue, hands that shed innocent blood, a heart that plots wicked schemes, feet eager to run to evil, a lying witness who gives false testimony, and one who stirs up trouble among the brothers.—Proverbs 6:16-19

READ: ROMANS 12:1-18

Hate is a strong word. It can be described as passionately or intensely disliking something or someone. To hate means to absolutely, positively, no-way-around-it, get-out-of-here disapprove of something.

When God says He hates something, it's very important to slow down and listen to His warning about what that something is. Since God so loved the world that He sent His only Son, Jesus, to die for us, it means that Jesus paid a big price for our sins—such as when we lie, plan trouble, or argue. Solomon was wise enough to ask about these things, and God gave him a list of sins that He absolutely does not tolerate. He actually said He hates them.

Here they are: pride, lying, murder, planning evil, excitement at doing wrong, lying about someone on purpose, and stirring up trouble with the people around you. Wow.

If those are seven things that hurt God's heart the most, then it makes no sense to do them. If He dislikes them intensely, there must be big consequences that come from acting them out. Can you think of how it would make someone feel if you lied about them? Or planned to do something mean to them? It would not end in anything good. It would only be hurtful and unkind.

So, let's make sure to heed this warning and love what Jesus loves instead.

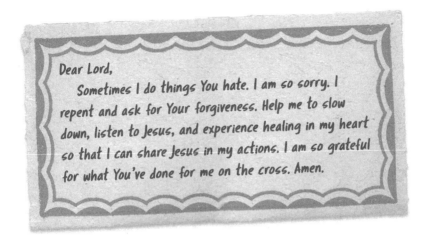

Dear Lord,
    Sometimes I do things You hate. I am so sorry. I repent and ask for Your forgiveness. Help me to slow down, listen to Jesus, and experience healing in my heart so that I can share Jesus in my actions. I am so grateful for what You've done for me on the cross. Amen.

Hearing things that God hates can make us a little sad. Maybe you even struggle with doing some of the things He hates. We all do at times.

Thankfully, Jesus came to help us! He came to save us, not only by His blood but also by His example of kindness and love. Look at the seven sins listed in the reading. Can you think of the opposite of those seven sins? For example, if God hates lying, then He must love the truth!

Go through each sin, and write out the opposite of its ugliness. Pray and ask God to help you do good work, and practice doing what God loves. He will give you strength and joy while you do!

_____

_____

_____

_____

_____

_____

27

DON'T STRAY

Don't let your heart turn aside to her ways; don't stray onto her paths.—Proverbs 7:25

READ: PROVERBS 7

You're minding your own business when a delicious scent wafts in from the kitchen. Warm, sweet, cocoa-y goodness fills the air. Like a zombie, your feet blindly follow the smell until you see it: a pan full of chewy, chocolatey brownies. You reach out in a dreamlike state, but suddenly—

"Wait! They have to cool first!" You snap out of it long enough to see Mom set her pot holders on the counter and walk away.

Your eyes glaze back over. The smell of sweet cocoa now completely envelopes you, pulling you closer. You reach out in one quick movement, scoop up a handful, and shove the gooey chocolate into your mouth.

"Yeow! Pbth!" You spit out the molten lava. What looked and smelled like deliciousness just scalded your hand and your tongue. You won't taste anything for a week now! Much less brownies!

There's nothing wrong with eating brownies. But sometimes temptation can cause us to "turn aside" or "stray," as Solomon says, from the path we're supposed to be on, from the wisdom we've been given. That's why there are guidelines to follow, even with something so yummy. Don't eat cocoa straight out of the container, because it's bitter and dry. Don't eat raw batter, because the eggs could make you sick. And you certainly want to wait until the brownies cool before digging in.

Today, the temptation is brownies. Tomorrow, it will be something else. The point isn't in the temptation itself; it's in how you respond. When Mom or God or Solomon gives you guidelines, sure, you can choose to ignore them. But accepting the guidance of those wiser than you will help to keep you on the path of wisdom, of safety, of a full and Godly life.

Dear God,

Thank You for the rules You've set in place to keep me safe. And thank You for all the wise counselors who remind me of those rules. Help me to be strong as I face temptation, whatever the temptation may be. And help me to practice turning away from temptation now so that when more difficult situations arise, I'll be ready to face them with confidence. Thank You for sharing Your wisdom and Your strength. Amen.

Think of something you know how to do well: math problems or riding a bike or braiding hair. Write or draw step-by-step instructions, including any warnings for what not to do. What are the results if someone follows the directions? What are the results if they don't? Try it out on a friend or family member and see how they do!

28

WISDOM CALLING!

Listen, for I speak of noble things, and what my lips say is right. For my mouth tells the truth, and wickedness is detestable to my lips. All the words from my mouth are righteous; none of them are deceptive or perverse.
—Proverbs 8:6–8

READ: PROVERBS 8

When you hear a really interesting or smart person speak, don't you want to listen? I do!

In this passage in Proverbs, the writing comes from the point of view of Wisdom herself, as if she's a character in the story. "She" sets the stage to tell readers of the Bible all the things that are important, fair, smart, and right. The beginning of the chapter starts by her calling out into the streets of the world with her voice, waiting for someone to listen and respond.

She goes on to express that she speaks of "noble things," which is information kings and queens should know. And you know what? God says that His believers are His royal sons and daughters (1 Peter 2:9). So Wisdom is speaking to us as royalty. With a calling like that, it's important that we know exactly what she is saying. Her advice is straight from God Himself.

As Proverbs 8 describes, Wisdom was with God from the very beginning! You'll want to read her full chapter to catch a glimpse of her beauty. Wisdom loves the truth and hates wickedness. Knowing what Wisdom is and what it isn't is becoming a very important theme throughout our journey through Proverbs. Thankfully, the Bible is giving us some good lessons to think about!

> Dear Lord,
> Thank You for sharing Your book of wisdom—the Bible—with me. It has so many answers to so many of my heart's questions. Help me to grow my hunger for reading Your Word and learning the important and "noble" things it has to tell me. I am grateful for Your instructions. Amen.

If you could ask Wisdom anything at all, what would it be? You might not be able to ask "Wisdom" directly, but I bet you have some wise people in your life. Maybe it's a family member, a grandparent, a pastor, or a teacher.

Take some time today to list some of the questions you have about God, the Bible, or the best way to live. Be sure to think through things you might be struggling with or unsure about. Then, make a phone call or set up a time to interview a wise person in your life! Try to get a variety of answers on different topics; these interviews are a great way to understand many perspectives with wisdom.

29

WISE OR FOOLISH?

"Whoever is inexperienced, enter here!"–Proverbs 9:4

READ: PROVERBS 9

Proverbs 9 is like getting two different invitations in the mail.

One invitation reads: "Feeling behind? Needing guidance? Please join us for fresh-baked goodies at my house. We'll help you learn everything you need to leave foolishness behind!"

The other starts the same, but . . . "Feeling behind? Needing guidance? We'll sneak into the bakery and take all their goodies. Then I'll show you *all* the tricks you need to get ahead."

You've probably never gotten invitations like that in the mail. But you probably *can* relate to the two different invitations from Wisdom and Folly (or Foolishness). Both are offering help, but in very different ways that will lead to very different results.

Wisdom has carefully built her house and planned her meal. She invites you to search for understanding. She warns of the danger of mockery and wickedness. And she reminds us, "The fear of the LORD is the beginning of wisdom" (v. 10).

But Folly is "rowdy," believes everything she hears, and doesn't try to learn anything (v. 13). She sits around whooping and yelling at people, inviting those who know no better to join her for "stolen water" and bread that's eaten in secret (v. 17).

You may not realize it, but you get those invitations every day. Want to be beautiful? Want to have the coolest stuff? Want to get rich quick? Want to make the best grades? Want everyone to like you? Want to live an easy life of success?

There's nothing necessarily wrong with the invitations themselves. But before accepting any of them, be sure to know who they're from. The difference could be a life lived with Wisdom or a life lived with Folly.

Dear Lord,
    Please help me to sort out the invitations I'm hearing daily. Help me to hear the voice of Wisdom when she calls. And help me to recognize when it's Folly inviting me into foolishness. Encourage me to spend time in Your Word so that I can easily spot the difference between the two. Thank You for Your all-knowing, ever-present guidance. Amen.

Write down some of the "invitations" you've heard lately from friends, teachers, videos, or commercials inviting you to learn more about something. After you write down everything you can think of, circle the invitations that seem to be from Wisdom. Cross out the invitations that seem to be from Folly. Going forward, with every invitation you receive, use that same process, even if you're only circling and crossing them out quietly in your mind.

30

DILIGENT HANDS

Idle hands make one poor, but diligent hands bring riches.
—Proverbs 10:4

READ: PROVERBS 10:1-10

How do you spend your time each day? How much free time do you have? Most adults would probably say they are really busy. Kids often say they are busy one day but bored the next. Schedules can be overwhelming, and life can feel like it moves fast during busy seasons. But what about the boring moments in between? If we take a close look at every minute of every day, we might see that we waste a lot more time than we think.

Now, let me be clear: rest is good and holy and necessary. The Bible actually tells us to save one day of rest each week and to "keep it holy" (Exodus 20:8). Some people use this day to nap or do something enjoyable. Rest is necessary for our health, and the amount of rest you need changes as you grow. If you aren't already getting enough sleep and taking a day of holy rest, those are definitely two things to *add* to your to-do list.

What about the rest of your day? Is there time you simply waste? Do you mindlessly stare at the TV? Do you spend way too much time arguing with a brother or sister? Do you scroll and scroll and scroll on your tablet? It's good to evaluate how you spend your time! If an activity doesn't contribute something good to your life, or if you spend more than a reasonable amount of time on it, maybe you should take another look at how you experience your day.

Proverbs 10:4 warns us about having hands that are "idle" (not productive) and tells us of the rewards of "diligent hands." *Diligent* doesn't mean that we're going full blast, spending every single second working and wearing ourselves out. But it does mean that we are careful and intentional in what we do. We think about how we spend our time and do it on purpose, with purpose.

Spend some time thinking about how you spend your time, with the goal to have "diligent hands."

Dear God,

Thank You for the gift of each and every day. Please help me to use the minutes and hours of my days wisely—for the purposes You have for my life. Please help me to be aware of the ways I may waste my time, and help me to put that time to work for You. Amen.

So let's look at exactly how we spend our time. For one day, take notes for each hour, trying to account for every minute of the day. Write down when you wake up (8:00—Woke up) and the time you spent getting ready (8:00-8:15—Got dressed), and continue that throughout the entire day.

When you're finished, look back at how you spent your time. Did keeping track of it help you to stay on task, to use your time more wisely? Did you notice large amounts of time being wasted? Do this activity as often as you need in order to be more diligent with your days.

31

LIKE A FOUNTAIN

The mouth of the righteous is a fountain of life, but the mouth of the wicked conceals violence. Hatred stirs up conflicts, but love covers all offenses.—Proverbs 10:11-12

READ: 1 CORINTHIANS 13:4-7

Have you ever said something you wish you hadn't? Maybe you hurt your friend's feelings, or perhaps you were mean to your brother or sister. Or maybe you even said something to your mom or dad when you knew you shouldn't have. How did you feel after you said what you did?

Most likely you didn't feel very good after you were rude or hurtful. The Bible says the words that come out of our mouths are very powerful. They can speak life, like a "fountain" of goodness, or they can bring "destruction" (Proverbs 10:11, 14).

Whoa.

In one expression, you can bring a person encouragement, or you can bring them sadness. It all comes down to the *choice* to speak something good or speak something bad.

The next time you have a choice to use your voice for good, do it! Even if you feel like saying something hurtful, make yourself pause and *turn the negative into a positive*. If you do, your words will be like a fountain of life to someone who needs it instead of a rude voice that can hide anger inside. It's your choice; make it a good one!

> Dear God,
> I want to make good choices with the words I say. Help me to practice self-control by thinking before I speak. Help me to be a voice for good and not for evil. I want my words to bring people goodness and not destruction, life and not death. Amen.

Practice kindness on purpose today! Your goal is to speak life to every person you see in the next 24 hours. Can you do it? Yes, you can!

For one day, focus on others *on purpose*. Use your voice to give every person you see a nice compliment. You can tell them what you like about what they are wearing, how they have a great smile, something you love about them, or just that you love and care about them! At the end of the day, write down a few of your favorite responses to the kind words you spoke.

Make sure you notice how you feel at the end of the day! Was it a good day or a bad one? Most likely it looked like a full, happy, tall fountain, and that makes anyone feel special.

_____

_____

_____

_____

_____

_____

_____

_____

_____

32

SMART TALK

Wisdom is found on the lips of the discerning, but a rod is for the back of one who lacks sense. The wise store up knowledge, but the mouth of the fool hastens destruction.
—Proverbs 10:13–14

> **READ: PROVERBS 10:13–21**

To discern means to recognize whether something might be right or wrong. It means that you listen well, take a step back, and look at a problem from all angles before trying to speak about it.

When one of your parents or a teacher catches you doing something that might look like trouble, what usually happens? Do they take a minute to ask you a few questions before accusing you of wrongdoing immediately? Or does the conversation go to trouble right away?

And what about you? If you see friends doing something you aren't sure about, do you give them a minute to explain, or do you get really mad before knowing all the information? It can be easy to see something confusing, make a judgment in our brain right away, and then forget to give grace in our speech. But Solomon reminds us that wisdom is found in people who look at a problem from all angles before speaking or reacting with anger. He also says that when we lack common sense, it's time for correction!

Slowing down before you speak can help you better react to a situation. Maybe your brother asked permission before eating that last piece of pie. Maybe the coach told your teammate to move positions, and you didn't know it. It's important to remember that taking the time to *listen well* and *speak with grace* are always better options.

Dear Jesus,
    Please help me remember to listen well and speak with grace. Put a guard over my mouth when it's not time to speak up, and give me the patience to listen for Your instructions with humility. I want to serve You with my words and my actions. Amen.

Grab a narrow strip of paper, and simply write "Go," "Stop," and "Slow" in a column.

"Go" means you feel free, clear, and confident. "Slow" means you're struggling, thinking, or currently working through something. "Stop" means it's time to breathe, take a break, and pull yourself together for a few minutes.

When you're really angry about something or struggling with God over a situation that seems unfair or difficult, put a paper clip on which word represents your emotions.

If it's a tough situation, start with "Stop," and place the paper clip there. Take several deep breaths and let out your emotions through journaling, exercise, or prayer. Then move your paperclip to "Slow" once you're in the "discerning" stage and can think more clearly about the problem at hand. Keep breathing and processing your thoughts by prayer or even talking to yourself out loud.

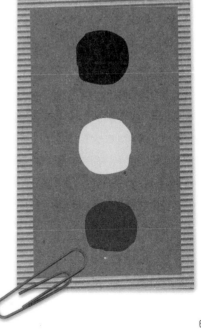

If you need more help, find a Bible verse to help your thoughts line up with God's Word. When your mind feels good and clear, move that paper clip to "Go." Even though you're young, it's a great time to develop self-control and learn to speak truth in a smart way!

FREEDOM

The righteousness of the upright rescues them, but the treacherous are trapped by their own desires.—Proverbs 11:6

READ: PROVERBS 11:6-15

At some point in your life, you'll probably hear someone say that the rules of the Bible are too old and out-of-date and that they are just a list of rules that limit us.

Rules like: Don't make fun of people. Don't run around with sketchy people. Don't pick fights with people. Don't be jealous of your neighbor. Don't worship anything other than God. Don't be ugly to your parents. Don't, d-don't, don't, don't.

But imagine for a moment a life where you were free, even encouraged, to do all those things. What would that life look like if you replaced each *don't* with *do*? Go back and read it that way.

Is that the type of world you want to live in? Especially when you're on the receiving end of all the making fun and sketchiness and picking fights and jealousy and ugliness? Nope. No, thank you. Absolutely would not.

As Jesus said it, "Truly I tell you, everyone who commits sin is a slave of sin. . . . If the Son sets you free, you really will be free" (John 8:34, 36). I much prefer a world where we look for the wisdom and knowledge of God and try to live up to it. And we do it even knowing we will never live up to that standard of holiness, but also knowing that there's the grace of Jesus Christ, who died on the cross to cover it all.

Solomon's wisdom here in Proverbs 11 is the same wisdom that Jesus shared hundreds of years later because God's truth doesn't change. Don't let Satan twist it. God's truth is the only truth. And the only true freedom is in a life that follows Christ.

○○ ○○○ ○○○ ○○○ ○○○

> Dear Jesus,
>   Thank You for dying on the cross so that we may have a life of freedom. Help me never to take that sacrifice and this gift of life for granted. Help me to respect the rules of Your Word and follow Your way, not the ways of this world, so that I may always find freedom in You. Amen.

We've heard a lot of *don'ts* from the wise King Solomon so far. And you've probably heard some from other parts of the Bible too. (See Exodus 20 for the Ten Commandments.) Think about those *don'ts* and choose the one that is the hardest for you to follow or understand. Write it out here. Then underneath, list the ways it restricts you, and list all the ways that it helps you to be free.

_____

_____

_____

_____

_____

_____

SOLOMON SAYS: *Go to pages 22, 36, and 44 to see some of Solomon's don'ts.*

34

PIG SNOUTS

A beautiful woman who rejects sense is like a gold ring in a pig's snout.—Proverbs 11:22

READ: ISAIAH 61

What comes to mind when you think of the word *beautiful*? Maybe you think of a movie star's photogenic face and how it represents the way the world defines *beauty*: famous and powerful with the "perfect" physical look to make it to the big screen. But does the Bible define loveliness the same way? Does Solomon tell us to value this kind of beauty? Nope.

In today's Scripture, Solomon says that a beautiful woman who is foolish and doesn't use good sense is no more beautiful than a ring in a pig's snout. Whoa! That's a pretty bold statement, don't you think? When the most gorgeous golden ring is hanging from a muddy pig's snout, we only see the pig.

God gives each of us amazing beauty, gifts, and talents. We need to realize that foolish choices and senseless living will overshadow all our gifts, no matter how beautiful. Wisdom and God's glory are what make people attractive. When you focus on showing the world your kind heart, your generosity, and your joyful spirit, no pig will be able to steal your spotlight, and your inner and outer beauty will shine for God.

So as you make decisions each day, remember this lesson. Using good sense shows your best to the world, and not using your smarts takes you straight to the farm. *Oink, oink!*

✣ ✣ ✣ ✣ ✣ ✣

Dear Jesus,

You are the most beautiful person there is. Please give me the strength to be like You in my thoughts and desires and in my words and actions. I want people to see You when they look at me. Amen.

Have you ever visited a farm or a zoo and seen a pig in real life? Even if you haven't, ask your parents to help you search online for information about pigs. Notice all the features of a pig in the mud. What do they eat? Do they exercise? Do they make noise? How do they smell?

Now picture a beautiful gold ring. Do you think it would be better to give the ring to a person, or give a pig the gold ring to put in its snout?

It seems like a waste to decorate the pig, doesn't it? Don't waste your talents and beauty by not using sense!

35

LOOKIN' FOR TROUBLE

The one who searches for what is good seeks favor, but if someone looks for trouble, it will come to him.—Proverbs 11:27

READ: DEUTERONOMY 30:15-27

Have you ever heard someone say, "He's just lookin' for trouble"? When you go looking for trouble, guess what you find. Trouble, right? It seems so simple. Why would anyone ever, on purpose, go *looking* for trouble? And yet . . .

How many times have you done something that you knew was wrong before you even did it? You're not alone. It's called sin, and it's as old as Adam and Eve. Paul said it like this in Romans: "I don't really understand myself, for I want to do what is right, but I don't do it. Instead, I do what I hate" (Romans 7:15 NLT). Can you relate?

The thing that Solomon is saying in Proverbs 11:27 and *the* thing to remember is: you have a choice. Even if that bad thing sounds super exciting, you can say no. Even if that good thing sounds really, really hard, you can say yes. And with every yes and no, you are making a decision about the kind of life you will lead, about the kind of person you will be. We can lead lives of purpose, searching for good, looking for the next right thing to do. Or we can go looking for trouble and, well, find it.

It's up to you.

Dear Jesus,

You are perfect. You have never sinned. And yet You paid the price for my sins. Please help me to honor You by choosing to walk away from sin and, instead, walk toward the good, toward You. Amen.

Have you ever played Red Light, Green Light? Play it with your family or a few friends. (You'll need at least three people.)

One person is the caller, and the others stand side by side. The caller will face the others, but stand far away, within hearing distance, from the others and call out, "Green light!" The players will walk toward the caller, and the caller, when she chooses, will say, "Red light!" If any of the players are still moving after the caller says "red light," that player is out. The caller continues alternating between "red light" and "green light" until everyone is out or until the first player reaches the caller. The first player to reach the caller wins!

This game can be so much fun. But it can also remind you of your choices between right and wrong—what we choose to do with the red lights and the green lights in our lives. When you have a choice to make, try to think of it as a red light (a bad choice) or a green light (a good choice). If it's a red light, *don't do it*, and wait until a green light shows you where to go.

FLOURISHING

Anyone trusting in his riches will fall, but the righteous will flourish like foliage. The one who brings ruin on his household will inherit the wind, and a fool will be a slave to someone whose heart is wise. The fruit of the righteous is a tree of life, but a cunning person takes lives.
—Proverbs 11:28–30

READ: PSALM 52

Solomon makes three very important points in this passage in Proverbs. To break it down simply, he says: trusting in money will fail you, bringing harm to your family will cause a storm, and fools will always serve the wise. Wow! Those are really clear statements.

First things first, money can't save us. As important as it is to save up money from a job well done, it's more important to understand that Jesus is the one who saves us. Money is a tool we can use to help steward the gifts God has given us, but it can never replace the relationship God has with us. Knowing the difference teaches us not to get caught up in trying to be rich because then we often miss out on God.

Second, treating our family members with truth, love, and kindness brings peace to our lives, but stirring up trouble causes a storm to rise. Do you prefer peace or a storm? Peace sounds like a better deal!

Solomon goes on to say that those who make good decisions can give away life, while those who try to cause division or trouble will end up stealing from others. Can you think of ways you can give away life? Perhaps you can share with your siblings, do the dishes for Mom, or give your dad a big hug. You might also want to say a prayer for the neighbors or take your dog for a walk! There are a lot of simple ways to flourish in righteousness.

Choose wisely.

Dear God,

I want to trust You more than riches. I want to trust in You at all times and learn how to use money wisely. Help me to treat my relationships with peace and wisdom, as they also teach me how to build my relationship with You. Amen.

Which one of these three topics do you struggle with the most? Trusting in money? Bringing harm to your family? Or making foolish choices? Write down the part of the Bible verse that matches the topic you want to work on.

Say a prayer asking God to help you with this lesson. Tell Him examples where it has been hard in your life, and ask Him to give you some opportunities to practice in a better way.

After you are finished talking with God, tell a parent, sibling, or friend what you are learning and practicing. Ask the person to check in with you in a week or so to see how it's going! Perhaps he or she will want to choose one of the three verses to work on as well. That's the power of wisdom, prayer, and friendship all in one.

37

DEEP ROOTS

Wickedness never brings stability, but the godly have deep roots.—Proverbs 12:3 NLT

READ: PROVERBS 12:1-12

Have you ever seen the "helicopters" drop from a maple tree? Much like leaves in the fall, these tiny whirligigs rain down from maple trees in the spring. As kids, we would gather as many as our little hands could hold, throw both handfuls in the air, and watch the swirly, twirly cloud fall all around us.

You may notice, if you look at these helicopters closely (or if you peel them apart like we did), a tiny, green seed at the point of the helicopter wing. It's the whole point of the aerodynamic design: to help these little seeds fly far from their parent trees and plant themselves in the dirt. And if you keep watching them, you'll notice that after these guys fall to the ground, the ones that find a nice patch of dirt will sprout a tall chute with a baby maple leaf on top.

Some of those seedlings will pop up in a crevice in the driveway and get washed away by the first hard rain. Some will grow in the middle of the lawn and disappear when the grass is mowed. But some of them, if left alone to grow, will push their tendrils deep into the soil and grow into a tall, strong maple tree. It's all in the roots.

With only tiny roots in shallow soil, the seedlings will simply wash away. But with strong roots, a maple tree will grow strong enough for you to lean against, strong enough to climb, even strong enough to hold a tree house.

Think about your roots. What is feeding them? Where are you planted? And what are you growing into?

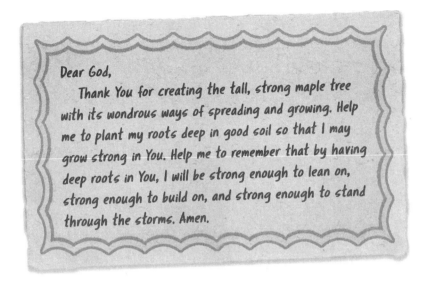

Dear God,
    Thank You for creating the tall, strong maple tree with its wondrous ways of spreading and growing. Help me to plant my roots deep in good soil so that I may grow strong in You. Help me to remember that by having deep roots in You, I will be strong enough to lean on, strong enough to build on, and strong enough to stand through the storms. Amen.

Have you heard the parable of the sower? Read Jesus' parable in Matthew 13:18–23. Then divide a piece of paper into three sections. Draw plants growing in the three different types of soil described in the passage. Then write life examples that are present in each type of soil. (For example, in the thorns, you could write "worry.") What can you do to make sure your roots are growing in good soil?

38

A MOUTH FULL OF FRUIT

A person will be satisfied with good by the fruit of his mouth, and the work of a person's hands will reward him.
—Proverbs 12:14

READ: PROVERBS 12:13–23; GALATIANS 5:22–23

Remember when we talked about the fruit of the Spirit in devotion 23?

The book of Galatians shares the nine characteristics that are proof of God's life in ours: *love, joy, peace, patience, kindness, goodness, gentleness, faithfulness,* and *self-control.* Our proverb today also talks about fruit, but it relates to the words we speak. Solomon says the good words of our mouths (what we say) as well as the work of our hands (our practical actions) are what bring satisfaction and reward. That's a pretty good deal if you think about it! It's amazing that both speaking well and working hard are gifts of God. He made us with a voice, and He gave us a purpose. When we use our voices well and when we do the work He's called us to, we end up feeling good in our hearts also.

This goes to show that what we say and do are of the utmost importance! The little things in our day-to-day life are the way we learn how to be and walk like Jesus. He has always been very careful with His words; they are even highlighted in red in some Bibles! We can show Him how grateful we are by choosing to speak to others with goodness and working hard at all we do.

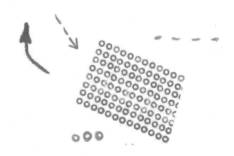

Dear Jesus,

    Thank You for opportunities to speak with kindness! Help me to always use my voice in a way that pleases You and to work with my hands in a way that honors You. I want to live out these actions as a reflection of Your heart living through mine. Amen.

Grab seven index cards from the junk drawer at your house! (You have one, don't you?)

    On each of the seven cards, write out a compliment that any person might like to receive, such as, "You are kind," "You are a hard worker," or "You are smart." Throughout the week, pull out one of the cards and think about who you can bless with that compliment this week. Then follow through. Enjoy the process of speaking a good word to others on purpose!

Kindness → PATIENCE

Joy Self-Control

Gentleness

Faithfulness PEACE

LOVE Goodness

SOLOMON SAYS: Go to page 50 to read more about the fruit of the Spirit.

39

A GOOD WORD

Worry weighs a person down; an encouraging word cheers a person up.—Proverbs 12:25 NLT

 READ: PROVERBS 12:24–28

Here, Solomon describes exactly what worry feels like: a weight on your mind, in your stomach, in your heart. Recent studies have shown that worry doesn't only affect your brain, but over time, anxiety can weaken your organs,* which sounds a lot like it *literally*, physically, weighs a person down.

So how do we avoid that? We can't just avoid everything that makes us nervous or causes us to worry. But we surely don't want worry hijacking our brain and taking our other organs with it.

Our buddy Solomon offers a simple, effective remedy: a good word. No, seriously. If worry starts in the brain, we can work on it right there, by changing the words in our head and the way we think. Of course, we can head off the nervousness in the first place with preparation, like for a test or a big trip. But when the test or trip is here and you're still worrying and weighed down, we can lighten the load by replacing those nervous thoughts with good ones.

Of course, the best word of all is God's mighty Word. It "is living and effective and sharper than any double-edged sword" (Hebrews 4:12). And it can most certainly be the "encouraging word" that cheers up a worried heart.

Here are a few to tuck in your brain:

- "Do not be afraid or discouraged, for the LORD your God is with you wherever you go." (Joshua 1:9)
- "Don't worry about anything, but in everything, through prayer and petition with thanksgiving, present your requests to God." (Philippians 4:6)
- "Even when I go through the darkest valley, I fear no danger, for you are with me." (Psalm 23:4)

The next time you're feeling worried, nervous, or just weighed down, fill that heavy heart up with encouraging words and just see how much lighter it feels!

---

* https://centerforanxietydisorders.com/stress-affects-child-development/

Dear God,

Thank You for Your mighty Word. Help me to keep it in my mind and heart and to use it whenever I'm weighed down. Help me to remember always to bring my worries to You and to rely on Your promises to calm them. Amen.

What worries you? What makes you nervous? Write it all down in one column on the left. Then, in the column on the right, write a Bible verse, "an encouraging word," to answer those worries and fears. Anytime you feel your heart growing heavy, encourage your heart with these words.

WORRY	BIBLE VERSE
✚	
✚	
✚	
✚	
✚	
✚	
✚	
✚	
✚	
✚	
✚	
✚	
✚	
✚	
✚	
✚	
✚	

40

LISTEN WELL

A wise son responds to his father's discipline, but a mocker doesn't listen to rebuke.—Proverbs 13:1

READ: PROVERBS 13:1-3

It's not fun being disciplined, is it? No one loves fixing messes or making up for something they did wrong. Sometimes it can feel frustrating, embarrassing, tiring, or just plain not fun. Needless to say, no one should enjoy doing wrong or being lazy either. It makes much more sense to be wise before finding yourself in a pickle, but that's just not always the case.

As humans, we will all mess up, need a course correction, need advice, or sometimes need even more discipline. (Ever had to run extra laps at a sports practice?) The good thing about it all, though, is that making mistakes and then working on discipline can make us better. When we listen—like, for real, listen—to how to correct some of our missteps, we will actually learn a lot.

Hebrews 12:6 even says that "the Lord disciplines the one he loves"; that means God can actually bring us closer to Him when we listen to His correction, even when it's sometimes difficult. In all reality, that's really loving! God could choose to turn away from us, but instead, He says to come closer to Him so that we can learn a better and more productive way. Even in correction, there is kindness and hope. What an awesome God!

DISCIPLINE

Dear God,

Thank You for loving me, even by Your discipline! Help me to receive Your love, correction, encouragement, and closeness. I want to live my life for You, in the way You know is best for me. Amen.

The next time you get into some trouble, take the discipline of your parents seriously (even if it's hard). As Solomon says, it's good to listen to correction and to gain wisdom in making better choices for the future.

But after that's all said and done, invite your parents to a "Let It Go Party," and that means PILLOW FIGHT! Who doesn't want to be disciplined with the glee of a gentle pillow to the face? Have some fun after the hard lesson, and remember that even in repair and readjustments, God always loves you. We become more like His image when we accept His guidance and rest in the joy of knowing He takes care of us. It's fun to be His child!

41

WALK WITH THE WISE

The one who walks with the wise will become wise, but a companion of fools will suffer harm.—Proverbs 13:20

READ: ROMANS 12:16

BFF. Friend Forever. Bae. Dude.

What word do you use to describe your best of friends? There are all kinds of nicknames to describe the people we are closest to. When we give someone a special name that only we get to use, it's a natural way to feel close to him or her. But one name we would not want to give a good friend is "fool." In today's verse, Solomon says we're much better off to walk with friends who are wise than with the foolish.

Back on page 13, you thought through a list of close friends and not-as-close friends. Solomon shared about how to choose friendships that are wise as well as how to grow those friendships. How is that going?

The reason we're talking about friendship again is because Solomon brings it up again! Isn't that what your parents do when something is really important? He must think that choosing the right types of friends is pretty important too! So give yourself a minute, and turn back to page 13 to review your circle of friendships.

Is your list of friends the same today? Have you added any new friends, or have any of your friendships changed much since you last wrote down your circles? It's a good idea to review this list from time to time because it reminds us that Solomon's instruction says to "walk with the wise to become wise." You don't want disaster to follow after you; that would stink! Instead, let good find you by walking with friends who are moving in the same Godly direction.

Dear Jesus,
   Thank You for the gift of friends. I ask that You would help me choose good friends while I am learning and growing. Please help me to be kind, compassionate, gracious, and loving while spending time with others who are too. Amen.

It's pretty clear that hanging out with wise friends will also make you wise! Can you think of any other Godly characteristics that you look for in a good friend? Write those characteristics down. It's good to have them in mind when looking for new friends. What are some characteristics that could sway you into foolishness? Write those down too. These can serve as a good reminder of what to avoid when navigating friendships.

42

REWARDS OF RIGHTEOUSNESS

Disaster pursues sinners, but good rewards the righteous.
—Proverbs 13:21

READ: PROVERBS 13:4–21

Have you ever been to one of those super-fun places where you earn a bunch of tickets playing games (Skee-Ball, anyone?!) and then cash in the tickets at the end of the night for some sort of prize? It's usually a whole lot of work (and money) for a little bitty reward, but still, it's pretty entertaining, and you get to go home with a souvenir too.

We've heard a lot about the rewards of wisdom and righteousness so far. And no doubt, we will continue to hear more. But unlike the rewards from those ticket places, the rewards from wisdom and righteousness are pretty huge and life-changing.

In this passage alone, just like the ticket prices on the prizes, we see the investment and the reward of a God-centered life.

- Work hard = Gain prosperity
- Live without blame = Get Godly guardians
- Take advice = Grow wise
- Work hard = Get wealth that grows
- Respect a command = Succeed

And that's just the beginning of the rewards for righteousness. Okay, so they may not sound as fun as candy or a bouncy ball, but these prizes are sure to last longer and to make a greater impact on your life and the world around you. And even better, these prizes are just as sure as the candy sitting under the "50 tickets" sign.

God's promises are true. His rewards are real. And a life of wisdom, although not always easy and not always fun, is a life full of God's sweet rewards.

Take a look at your habits and routines and the choices you're making. What kind of rewards are you racking up in your life?

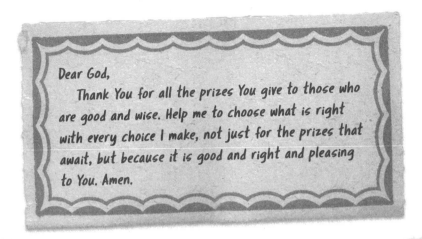

Dear God,
Thank You for all the prizes You give to those who are good and wise. Help me to choose what is right with every choice I make, not just for the prizes that await, but because it is good and right and pleasing to You. Amen.

Read through Proverbs 13:4-21, underlining or writing down the rewards that are promised to the wise, the hardworking, and the righteous. Make a list of each reward and the action associated with it. You may want to keep a running list as you continue to read through Proverbs—and even the whole Bible! Let the list remind you of life's big prizes, God's faithful promises, when you choose to live the way He created you to.

_____

_____

_____

_____

_____

_____

_____

SOLOMON SAYS: *Go to page 18 to read about the secret of success!*

LEAVE A LEGACY

A good man leaves an inheritance to his grandchildren.
—Proverbs 13:22

READ: PROVERBS 13:22-25

What's your legacy going to be? You're still young, at least compared to the grown-ups in your life, so you're probably thinking more about your next soccer game or next week's math test than you are about the legacy you're going to leave behind one day. But believe it or not, you've already started building that legacy.

A legacy isn't really about how much money or stuff you have. It's about how you've treated people. It's about the wisdom you've gained and shared. It's about the whole life you've built that will carry on after you're gone.

Think about your grandparents, for example. They built a life that will be their story once they're gone. What have they done for a career? How have they served others with their lives? What kind of family have they built? What kind of wisdom have they learned and shared with you? All these things together will create the legacy they leave behind.

When Solomon wrote Proverbs, he was already a father, thinking about what he would leave behind. He was probably thinking about the amazing legacy his father, King David, had left him: a wealthy, peaceful kingdom and a deep, rich faith. And it sounds like, from the passage above, that he had seen a legacy or two lost to bad decisions.

The truth is, you are never too old or too young to start building a legacy. You can treat everyone with kindness and respect. You can make choices to grow your faith each day. You can choose to listen and learn from your parents and teachers and grandparents so that you can build *your* legacy on theirs, reaching higher and stronger because of the wisdom they share with you. You can choose right now, today, to start leading a life, to start leaving a legacy, that you will be proud of.

Dear God,

Thank You for the wise and faithful people in my life. I am reading this book and talking to You right now because someone chose to share a legacy of faith with me. Please help me to be aware of the legacy that I am building and of the story my life will one day leave behind. Amen.

Have you ever seen a family crest? You can do a quick internet search for images (or ask an adult to), but they're basically the images you would see on a medieval soldier's shield or on the gate or flag of a castle. Draw the outline of a shield or a flag and design your crest by adding pictures of things that symbolize values that are the most important to you. You could hang a copy of the crest on your mirror or even draw it onto a T-shirt (with Mom's permission, of course) to remind you of the legacy that you are building every day.

44

THE HEART KNOWS

The heart knows its own bitterness, and no outsider shares in its joy.—Proverbs 14:10

READ: PROVERBS 14:1–11

*B*itter. It's another word for holding a grudge. And who likes that? No one I know! It's not fun to feel stuck, angry, or anywhere in between. There is no joy in bitterness, just a lot of sitting alone thinking and getting more and more upset. It can be unsafe for others to be close because that anger and bitterness often ends up bursting out onto someone else.

But if your heart is happy, it easily shares that happiness with others. It's like an overflowing cup of life and love, giving away joy to anyone who comes near. The heart knows what it is holding inside, and it shares with others from the inside out.

What do you do when you feel like your heart is hurt? Or angry? Do you let yourself get bitter? Do you have a safe place to go? Or a journal to write in? Do you go to your room to be alone, or do you talk to someone you trust about your feelings?

There are many helpful ways to handle a heart that is broken, disappointed, or frustrated. Expressing what is going on with your feelings in a way that is safe and truthful can open your eyes to seeing God's love in a whole new way. By writing your thoughts in a journal, talking with a trusted adult, or getting your emotions out through exercise, you might find a healthy way to avoid bitterness and focus on God instead.

> Dear God,
>   Thank You for loving my heart when it's sad, disappointed, or frustrated. Help me not to allow my feelings to turn to bitterness but to instead turn into joy. Please give me peace in knowing You can turn my brokenness into something good I can share with others. Amen.

Exercise makes the heart grow stronger! It might seem like a funny activity to go along with a bitter heart, but few things are better to fuel your joy than to get your blood pumping. Start today by doing a few jumping jacks, running laps up and down the street, or doing some sit-ups and push-ups. Stretch your back and your legs, and take a few deep breaths.

Whether your cup is overflowing from frustration or joy, movement helps! If exercising isn't a regular part of your day, consider adding it. Even if it's just twenty jumping jacks a day, it's a great start. Exercise helps anger, sadness, and fear disappear; it also helps happiness to be born.

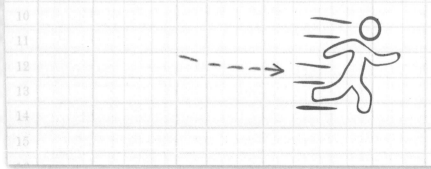

45

CAUTION!

The inexperienced one believes anything, but the sensible one watches his steps. A wise person is cautious and turns from evil, but a fool is easily angered and is careless.
—Proverbs 14:15–16

> **READ: PROVERBS 14:12–22**

Years ago, ago, a friend looked at me and said, "Did you know that the word gullible isn't in the dictionary?" (*Gullible* means that you'll basically believe anything anyone tells you.) I gasped and grabbed the dictionary off the shelf.

And then I realized the joke.

The word *gullible*, of course, is in the dictionary. Any reasonable person would know that. But a gullible person would believe that *gullible* is the one word that the wise dictionary editors left out. And the friend had a good laugh at my expense.

When you're young (even when you're a grown-up!), it's safe to say you're inexperienced at a lot of things. But that doesn't mean you have to be gullible. And you certainly don't need to be as old or wise as Solomon to be sensible. In fact, in the verses above, Solomon gives us three simple ways to do it.

1. **Watch your step.** Think about where you're going and what you're doing. Take each step with purpose and a plan. Face each day thinking about what's ahead of you.

2. **Be cautious.** When you see trouble ahead, stop and think. How can you avoid the trouble that's heading your way?

3. **Turn from evil.** Sometimes, even when you're cautious, bad situations are going to sneak up on you. Evil is going to whisper your name. Turn away from it, and turn directly to the holy God who loves you.

These three simple guidelines will help keep you on the path of a sensible life and keep you from running off the road in foolishness.

Dear God,

Thank You for all the times You've protected me in my inexperience. Help me to be more sensible by guiding my steps and reminding me to turn to You when I face troubles. Help me to learn from every mistake and misstep so that I will walk more closely with You. Amen.

Think about the types of street signs you see as you walk or ride down the street. Now design or draw your own signs for the three instructions on the left (and any other "cautions" or directions you can find in Proverbs 14:12-22). Hang them up to remind you of the many cautions Solomon has given you to guide you along the right path.

SOLOMON SAYS: Turn to page 62 for another proverb about being inexperienced.

46

LIFESAVING TRUTH

A truthful witness rescues lives, but one who utters lies is deceitful.—Proverbs 14:25

READ: PROVERBS 14:23-25

Think about all the professionals who save lives every day, such as lifeguards, doctors, firefighters, and ambulance drivers. You might assume you need to choose one of these careers to be a lifesaver yourself. But actually, Proverbs says you can rescue lives just by telling the truth. You don't have to be a firefighter or lifeguard to help someone by telling him the truth in a loving way. By simply living a life that represents the truth Jesus shares with us through His Word, you can be an everyday hero.

Now telling the truth can be a little tricky because sometimes people don't always want to know the truth. Believing a lie is sometimes more comfortable than believing what is right. And yet, if you can practice using a kind, gentle, and loving tone in your voice, people often receive the truth a lot easier! It can be as simple as slowing down before you speak or taking the time to understand a situation before saying your part.

Telling the truth isn't always the easiest thing to do, but it's the right thing to do! God gives us examples of people in the Bible, such as Jonah, who were afraid to lead by telling the truth, yet God gave them the courage to do so. Because He knows best! And the best is always the truth.

Dear God,

I want to be a truth-teller. Please give me the grace to tell the truth in a loving and kind way. Help me to be able to hear the truth, too, especially when I don't want to! Thank You for Your honesty always. Amen.

Let's take a look at some of the prophets of the Old Testament. The prophets were messengers who shared God's truth with people. Sometimes the message was very unpopular, and the people didn't want to hear it. But even so, God still filled the prophets with courage to speak the truth and share what was needed for the people to hear.

Most of the time, the prophets were telling people to repent or to change a bad behavior. Look in your Bible for the stories of Jonah, Moses, or Elijah. Find out more about how God used them to share messages of truth to save many people's lives. Which hero of faith is your favorite?

47

GOOD FEAR

In the fear of the LORD one has strong confidence and his children have a refuge. The fear of the LORD is a fountain of life, turning people away from the snares of death.
—Proverbs 14:26–27

READ: PSALM 34:11–22

The fear of the Lord, a healthy "fear" and awe of the Lord, is rewarding and beneficial and encourages great growth in our lives. Still, that concept, "the fear of the LORD," can be a difficult one to explain and grasp. So let's dig a little deeper and see how the Bible explains it.

Fear of the Lord is:

- Trying to please God, not men. (Colossians 3:22)
- Speaking truth and goodness. (Psalm 34:13)
- Turning from evil and doing good. (Psalm 34:14)
- Seeking peace. (Psalm 34:14)
- Finding joy in His commands. (Psalm 112:1)
- Standing in awe of Him. (Psalm 33:8)
- Trusting in Him, fearing nothing else. (Psalm 112:7–8)

It helps us by:

- Keeping us from sin. (Exodus 20:20)
- Making God attentive to our cries. (Psalm 34:15)
- Delivering us from our troubles. (Psalm 34:17)
- Giving us a "strong confidence." (Proverbs 14:26)
- Offering us life, protecting us from "the snares of death." (Proverbs 14:27)

As we've already learned, the fear of the Lord is the "beginning of knowledge" (Proverbs 1:7). So needless to say, it's an important concept not only to understand but also to build a life on. Take some time to really learn how to live each day with a healthy fear of the Lord in your life.

Dear Lord,

You are awesome. I know that. Help me to live my life in a way that shows my respect for Your power and glory. Help me to seek Your approval first, to seek peace, to turn from evil, to walk in Your ways. Help me to learn more about You and Your awesomeness so that my fear and awe of You will only grow. Thank You for protecting and delivering those who fear You, who worship You, who love You. Amen.

Look at the earlier list of seven things that describe what the fear of the Lord is. For the next seven days, choose one of those items to focus on each day. Write out each item or the Bible verse that goes with it to remind you of your goal for the day. Think of all the many ways you can bring that characteristic to life as you go about your day; then do them! When the week is finished, take a look at the other list, the list of ways in which the fear of the Lord helps us. How many of those things did you see happen during your week?

FOCUS!

SOLOMON SAYS: *Go to page 8 to read more about good fear.*

48

LOVE THE POOR

The one who oppresses the poor person insults his Maker, but one who is kind to the needy honors him.
—Proverbs 14:31

READ: PROVERBS 14:28-35

It's easy to want more, to buy more, to wish for more, isn't it? Sometimes, we are easily pulled into thinking that if we have all the material possessions we want, then we will be happy. But what happens when you get new shoes, the latest game, or a new basketball? Do you always use it for a long time? Or does it sometimes sit in the corner of your room once the next new thing arrives?

It can be a little of both. There is joy in receiving a new gift, and it's good to give thanks to God and to your parents for providing you with tools, sports equipment, and things that will help you grow and have fun. At the same time, it's also wise to consider what you can learn by having self-control, by choosing to forget about needing something new and think about serving someone instead.

You most likely have the food and clothes you need and even like. But what about a person across town who doesn't, whose family is poor and struggling to buy back-to-school supplies or enough food for everyone? Is there a way you could help with their needs instead of buying another thing that could just sit on your shelf? What if you keep using your backpack or shoes from last year and gift someone else the new purchases instead?

Solomon shares with us in this Proverb that those who are kind to the needy honor God. That means that God cares especially for the ones who are in need, and He is on their side! They are made in the image of Jesus just as much as anyone else on the planet.

So the next time it could be easy to buy yourself something to make you "happy" in an instant, take a minute to slow down and remember the poor. Consider purchasing a gift that would make someone else happy. Think about what you could learn in that moment about being kind to someone who needs that gift instead.

Dear Jesus,
   I'm sorry for the times I have been greedy or wanted more than I need. Please help me to remember the poor in prayer every day and to work for ways to help. I want to help others instead of only thinking about myself. Amen.

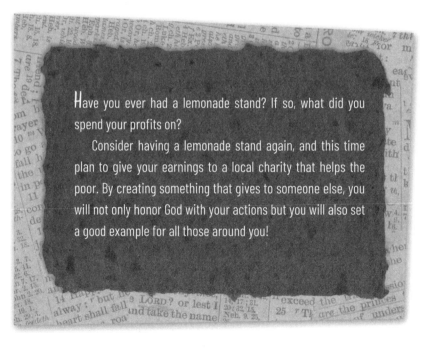

Have you ever had a lemonade stand? If so, what did you spend your profits on?

Consider having a lemonade stand again, and this time plan to give your earnings to a local charity that helps the poor. By creating something that gives to someone else, you will not only honor God with your actions but you will also set a good example for all those around you!

GENTLE ANSWERS

A gentle answer turns away anger, but a harsh word stirs up wrath.—Proverbs 15:1

READ: EPHESIANS 4:25-32

Are you starting to notice that a lot of these Proverbs have to do with how we treat others? Yeah, me too. Want to guess why?

Ephesians 4 tells us a lot about how to treat others, ending with "Be kind and compassionate to one another, forgiving one another, just as God also forgave you in Christ" (v. 32). You see, when we sign up to be Christ followers, when we accept His amazing gift of grace, when we call ourselves Christians, we become representatives of Christ. And the way we treat others becomes a part of the way people see Christ here on earth. His compassion, His forgiveness, and His love are how people will know we are His (John 13:35). We want to represent Him well by treating others the way He has treated us in His glorious grace.

But even more than that, God just wants us to be good to one another. He knows that's what is best for everyone, including us. He knows that kindness and compassion and gentleness are the healthiest ways for the human heart and mind to function.

A loud, angry word will only get a louder, angrier word in return. And soon you'll reach the point where both people are just shouting, unable to hear or understand what the other person is trying to say. It doesn't help the situation, and it most certainly doesn't represent who we are called to be in Christ.

So when you have a choice between harshness and gentleness, choose gentleness. Say something nice instead.

Dear Jesus,

It is so hard to answer an angry word with a nice one. But time and time again, You showed us how. Help me to look to Your examples of kindness and compassion and gentleness when mean words are thrown my way. Help me to look past the words and into the hearts of those who are hurting and answer them with the only thing that will heal them: Your love. Amen.

Emergency services recommend that your family have a plan for when there is a fire or other emergency in your home. So let's make a plan when you have an anger emergency, when fireballs of angry words are thrown your way. (And if you don't have a plan for an actual fire, you should do that too!)

Based on the wisdom Solomon gives above, create a plan for how to react to harsh or angry words. Is there a gentle answer you can give? Write out an example. Should you simply smile and walk away? Should you sometimes tell an adult? Maybe even end with a prayer asking God to help you forgive the person saying those angry words and to be an example of Christ's love for them. Create a plan for the best way to react in case of an anger emergency, and you can be ready for those harsh words thrown your way.

50

THE EYES OF THE LORD

The eyes of the LORD are everywhere, observing the wicked and the good.—Proverbs 15:3

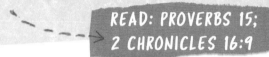

READ: PROVERBS 15;
2 CHRONICLES 16:9

Have you ever had someone watching you? Maybe when you were playing a sport, singing in your house, or taking a test. How did it make you feel?

It can probably feel several different ways depending on who is watching you. If it's your mom or dad, you likely feel safe and loved, connected and cared for. If it's the cheering fans of your team, you feel encouraged. When a coach or teacher watches you, you might feel the need to be careful and do your best. And if an audience has their eyes on you while you sing on stage, it can make you feel nervous!

No matter how it feels, being observed can be one of the best ways for us to grow. When we are watched by someone who cares about us, we can be assured that we are seen, valued, and important. We can also be encouraged or gently corrected. There's a better chance at everyone being honest and fair when someone is keeping a watchful eye, and it's easier for us to ask for and receive help. One of the ways we know God cares deeply for us is that He is always watching us! He sees us in our best behavior and also in our worst behavior. He knows how to celebrate us in just the way we need, and He also knows how to correct and comfort us with His Holy Spirit.

Because God always has His eyes on us, we know that we are safe and secure. By making good choices, walking in wisdom, and being kind, we can always give Him our best—even if no one else is watching. We can also always trust that He will bring justice when we've been hurt because He sees that too. Having God be present with us is the best company we can ask for!

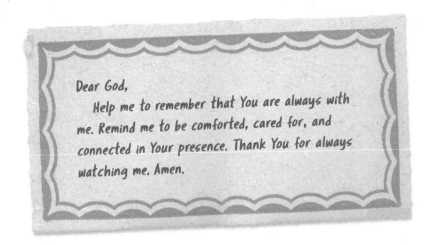

Dear God,
    Help me to remember that You are always with me. Remind me to be comforted, cared for, and connected in Your presence. Thank You for always watching me. Amen.

Cut a piece of paper into twenty small pieces. On each piece, write down an activity you did this week. Some examples might be: *soccer practice, homework, helped Dad, went to a birthday party.* Fold up each piece of paper, and put them all in a jar.

Take each piece of paper out one by one, and think about whether or not you sensed God's presence with you during that activity. As you answer the question for each activity, divide the pieces into "yes" and "no" piles. If your "yes" pile is larger, stop and thank God for making Himself known to you! If your "no" pile was the winner, stop and pray for a few minutes. Ask God to reveal Himself to you in new and everyday ways. Ask Him to open your ears and eyes throughout each day so that you can sense Him with you. Enjoy watching Him answer!

51

GOD'S PLANS > OUR PLANS

We can make our own plans, but the LORD gives the right answer. . . . Commit your actions to the LORD, and your plans will succeed.—Proverbs 16:1, 3 NLT

READ: PROVERBS 16:1-11

Imagine for a moment that you are the world's wisest leader. Imagine that God Himself told you that your wisdom would be unlike anyone before you or anyone to come (1 Kings 3:12). On top of that, you have a ridiculous amount of wealth. You are so wealthy that even silver is considered worthless (1 Kings 10:21). Are you holding your head a little higher? Standing a little taller? Feeling pretty proud of yourself?

If God had told *me* that *I* was the wisest in the world, I think I'd feel *preeetty* smart. But even with that, Solomon still points us back to the wisdom of God. Solomon knows that even as wise as he is, it is nothing compared to the omniscience—the all-knowingness—of God. Solomon knows that we can make all the plans in the world, but they'll go nowhere if God isn't behind them.

How often do you consider what God thinks about your plans, your dreams, your goals? Do you ask Him what He thinks? Do you think about the gifts He's given you? Do you ever just ask Him what plans *He* has for you?

Even if you don't hear Him speaking out loud to you, you can always hear His voice through the pages of your Bible. In Jeremiah 29:11, He tells the Jewish people, "For I know the plans I have for you . . . plans to prosper you and not to harm you, plans to give you hope and a future" (NIV). No matter how wise we think we are, God's plans are always bigger, always better. So before making any big plans for your life, just check in to see what God has in store.

Dear God,

Thank You for creating me for Your plans and purposes. I'm so grateful that You already know my future and that Your plans for me are good. Help me to remember to commit my plans to You, to seek Your wisdom in all of my plans, so that my plans in You will succeed. Amen.

Make a list of any life goals you have—little goals, big goals, any goals at all. Now take some time to see what God says about those goals. Look through His Word to see if you can find guidance, and say a prayer handing all your goals over to Him. If you repeat this prayer throughout life, you will be in the habit of committing all your plans to Him.

52

LEAD ON!

Better to be lowly of spirit with the humble than to divide plunder with the proud.—Proverbs 16:19

READ: PROVERBS 16:12–22

How would you define a good leader? Perhaps someone who is in charge of a task or maybe someone who is the best at what they do? A leader can be described in all sorts of ways. Leading can mean being in the front, or being responsible, or even being the one who works the hardest!

Being a leader also means practicing humility.

Hu-mil-i-ty. That's a big word to swallow.

Humility can be defined as making oneself less important than others. Or it also can mean not bragging about yourself . . . or not promoting yourself even if you know you are the best at a certain skill. It can be thinking of others more and thinking of yourself less. God says that it's wise to be humble.

Have you ever had a leader or teacher who acted like a proud, big boss or who tried to tell everyone what to do in a way that was unkind? If you have, I bet you didn't think it was any fun! His actions might have even hurt your feelings or made you angry.

Humble leaders, on the other hand, show kindness in their actions. When leaders choose to believe that others are more important than themselves, they can give people a gift like Jesus did. He always served people, taught with truth and kindness, and recognized the value in others. That's why He died for us! He chose the ultimate gift of humility, and He teaches us how to do the same.

The next time you have a chance to lead and catch yourself in a moment of bossiness or bragging, stop and remember Jesus' example of humility. Then lead on!

○○ ○○○ ○○○ ○○○ ○○○

Dear Lord,

Help me remain lowly in spirit when winning, losing, and everything in between. I want to have a heart and an attitude that resembles and honors You. In all things, let humility be one of the top expressions on my list of characteristics. Thank You for Your grace. Amen.

It's game time! Your challenge today is to choose two activities to practice. Pick one activity that you are really good at doing. Take the time to describe what you feel as you excel at this skill. Then pick one activity you have never tried or that you are not good at. Once again, take time to describe what it feels like to struggle with this skill. Find a friend who wants to join you. Encourage him along the way while you both learn something new together!

Let this activity serve as a good reminder that humility is always a good choice. We all can work on something, and it's important to be lowly of spirit instead of stealing someone else's joy.

53

THE WORDS OF OUR HEARTS

The heart of a wise person instructs his mouth; it adds learning to his speech.—Proverbs 16:23

READ: PROVERBS 16:23-33

Have you ever said something you didn't really mean? Or are you *always* saying things you wish you could take back? Always sticking your foot in your mouth?

Well, lucky for us, Solomon has the cure for foot-in-mouth disease. As we continue to listen to Solomon, to do as Solomon says, our hearts will grow wiser. And the words that come out of our mouths will grow wiser too.

Don't underestimate the power of this concept. First, you should know that Solomon isn't the only one trying to teach it to us. Hundreds of years after Solomon wrote these words in Proverbs 16:23, Jesus reminded us of the same, saying, "For the mouth speaks from the overflow of the heart" (Matthew 12:34). If God's own Son and the world's wisest king are trying to tell us something, it's probably a good idea to listen up.

Second, Jesus reminded us of the eternal impact of our words: "I tell you that on the day of judgment people will have to account for every careless word they speak. For by your words you will be acquitted, and by your words you will be condemned" (Matthew 12:36-37).

There's the saying, "Sticks and stones may break my bones, but words will never hurt me." But I don't think Jesus—or Solomon—would agree.

Our words are powerful. They can be helpful or hurtful. And they reveal the content of our hearts. If the words that come out of your mouth are not always what you would want them to be, pray the prayer of Solomon's father, David: "Search me, God, and know my heart" (Psalm 139:23). And God will help to cleanse your heart, along with the words overflowing from it.

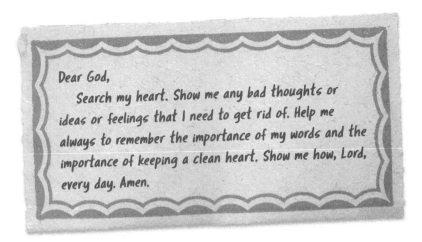

Dear God,

Search my heart. Show me any bad thoughts or ideas or feelings that I need to get rid of. Help me always to remember the importance of my words and the importance of keeping a clean heart. Show me how, Lord, every day. Amen.

In a journal or on a piece of paper, draw a heart. Then pray the prayer of David and ask God to search your heart. In the heart you drew, write any thoughts, ideas, or feelings that come to your mind. What do you see that is good and wise? What do you see that is bad or hurtful? Offer both up to God, thanking Him for the good and wise and asking Him to heal the bad and hurtful.

Every time you see a heart—on stickers or balloons or paper—let it remind you to pay attention to the words that come out of your mouth and how they reflect the feelings in your heart. Take them all to God with another prayer from David, "God, create a clean heart for me" (Psalm 51:10), knowing that God will listen and respond.

54

FAITHFUL WITH WHAT YOU HAVE

A prudent servant will rule over a disgraceful son and share an inheritance among brothers.—Proverbs 17:2

READ: PHILIPPIANS 4:8

Let's talk about the difference between two words. On one side we have *prudent*, meaning disciplined, neat, wise, or careful. On the other, we have *disgraceful*, meaning shameful, dishonoring, or unacceptable. I would say that is a pretty big difference! In fact, today's proverb tells us how these two characteristics can lead you in opposite directions.

Imagine a group of brothers, all expecting to share an inheritance one day. After all, they've been the rightful heirs since birth. But one of the brothers is lazy and disgraceful and brings dishonor to the family (bad choice, brother). Now imagine there's a servant. This guy was *not* born into the family, but he's prudent and hardworking. Because the servant has shown wisdom and discipline, he suddenly gets to step in, be in charge of the disgraceful son, and share in the inheritance. Way to go, servant!

So which guy would you rather be? The son who was born with tons of family perks but loses out because he is lazy and unreliable, or the faithful servant who has had to work hard but is well rewarded? When you look at the end result, the choice is easier.

You might have been born with some amazing advantages—a family to love you, as much food and rest as you need, teachers and books and a brain for learning. But if you don't appreciate and respect those gifts and use them well, you could miss out on so much that God has waiting for you.

On the other hand, maybe you've had to face some challenges, like a learning disability or financial difficulties in your family. Be encouraged by this proverb's message that diligence and wisdom can help you overcome your hurdles. God will support you in your efforts, especially if you are faithful with what you have. His inheritance will always be waiting for you.

Dear God,

Help me to work hard and to be faithful with what You have given me. Please give me the grace to choose wisely how to serve You and others. I want to be a person who is diligent, kind, pure, and wise. Amen.

Who doesn't like dessert? Spend today in the kitchen, baking a small batch of cookies or even something simple like pudding or gelatin (with whipped cream, of course!). While you're working in the kitchen and following the recipe, remind yourself that when you put the right actions and instructions forward, you come up with a wonderful treat. When the wrong things get added or if you aren't careful with your choices, you end up with a mess that no one wants to eat. Use this bake session as a reminder that we need to be wise with what God gives us, in and out of the kitchen!

55

EAR GUARDS

A wicked person listens to malicious talk; a liar pays attention to a destructive tongue.—Proverbs 17:4

READ: PROVERBS 17:4-9

Throughout Proverbs, Solomon has a lot to say about the *actions* of the wise and wicked. But in this verse we see that our wisdom is affected not only by what we do, but also by what we listen to.

We've talked about all the voices speaking into our lives. We've talked about what a difference they can make. So, how can we be sure that we only let in the good words, the wise words, the helpful words? Well, I'd say you need to get yourself a pair of ear guards.

You know how in soccer you throw your entire body across the net to keep the opponent's ball from getting in? Or how in air hockey you ferociously guard your goal to keep the puck from sliding through? Or how in volleyball you spike the ball that's trying to cross the net? How about we do that for our ears?

"Malicious talk"? Slam! Not getting in here! "Destructive tongue"? Spiked! Bad words, bullying, bragging? Take that and that and that! Not getting in these ears.

So when you hear someone at school saying mean things about the new kid, what do you do? Listen? Laugh? Or tell them to stop and walk away? There is no excuse for listening to bad things or "malicious talk," because Solomon says that only a wicked person will listen to stuff like that. Imagine what your family, your school, your *world* would be like if we all stopped speaking and listening to the negative, hateful, disrespectful talk. What a peaceful world this would be. Until then, from Solomon till today, the fight against foolish words continues. Of course, in the end, we know Jesus wins. But let's make sure that we're playing like we're on His team.

Dear Jesus,

Help me today and every day to guard my ears against malicious talk and destructive tongues. Help me to demolish arguments and take every thought captive, making it obedient to Your will. Help me to be a peacemaker, speaking and listening wisely, guarding my ears and guarding my heart. Amen.

Using only household items, create a table hockey game. You'll need a "puck" of some sort. It can be anything from a bottle cap to a paper wad. And you'll need a goal to try to shoot it in. A shoebox or basket would be perfect. To score, one person tries to slide the puck across the table and in the goal, while the other person protects the goal to keep the other person from scoring.

Play table hockey with a friend or family member, imagining the puck as those malicious words and the goal you're protecting as your ears, your heart. Then, as you go through this day, this week, put your ear guards to work and listen wisely, wherever you go.

SOLOMON SAYS: Go to pages 14, 44, 60, and 68 for more about listening and speaking in wisdom.

56

REBELS

An evil person desires only rebellion; a cruel messenger will be sent against him.—Proverbs 17:11

READ: PROVERBS 17:10-12; GALATIANS 6:7-8

You know those television shows that portray a person trying to make a difficult decision that may be risky? We see the person with an angel on one shoulder and a devil on the other, each messenger trying to convince the person to make the important choice. The angel is always encouraging the person to choose wisely, to think through right and wrong, and to follow through on what is good. On the other shoulder, the devil is trying to convince the person to make a bad choice, persuading them to believe it's not so bad, and giving them reasons to ignore the angel.

Even though you might not see an angel or a devil on your shoulder throughout your day, are there times when you get stuck in the middle of a tough choice? Perhaps one way seems a bit easier (but maybe not right), and the other way seems really hard, but it's the better choice.

Proverbs 17:11 offers wisdom for these hard-choice moments! "An evil person desires only rebellion; a cruel messenger will be sent against him." Solomon is saying that wrongdoers desire only to do more wrong, and the consequence of that is getting back what was sent. Yikes! That doesn't really make it too difficult to make the better choice instead, does it? If we get back what we send out, it seems wiser to send out something good and receive something good.

Can you think of a time when you did something wrong on purpose, and you then saw the consequence? How about when you did something good? It's important to know the difference!

Dear God,

Remind me of Your goodness every day. Give me wisdom to do good so that I can reap good. Give me strength to stand strong, to avoid rebellion, and to be a person who can tell the difference easily. Amen.

Take out a piece of paper and cut it into twenty pieces. On ten pieces, write activities that are life-giving, efficient, fun, productive, or wise. Perhaps you could eat cookies with friends, leave a nice note for someone, clean out your desk drawer, or sing a favorite song. On the other ten pieces, write things that are no fun (or unhealthy) to do such as eating too much dessert, sleeping until 2:00 p.m., being rude to a sibling, or stepping in doggie doo—eeww!

Fold the pieces closed, and place them in two separate bowls. Give one bowl to a friend or family member, and take turns taking one piece from the bowl and reading it aloud. Everyone then chooses which option seems like the better choice. It doesn't have to be super serious. Just have some fun, and laugh about making good choices over bad ones!

57

HOW TO STOP A FLOOD

To start a conflict is to release a flood; stop the dispute before it breaks out.—Proverbs 17:14

READ: PROVERBS 17:13–20

A flood usually doesn't come out of nowhere. First, you'll see clouds rolling in. Then raindrops will start to fall, one by one. The rain will grow heavier and heavier, filling the rivers until they spill out over their banks. It's then that we start to see the damaging effects of the flood.

As this proverb observes, conflicts usually work the same way. A bad attitude comes rolling in. Then, insults will fall, one by one. Irritation grows until it spills out in a flood of anger, damaging the people and relationships around us.

The good news is, as far as conflicts go, we can usually stop the flood. We can take notice when the stormy attitudes or rumors roll in. We can shine through those dark clouds with gentleness and kindness and truth. We can move to higher ground by refusing to participate in the negativity. And we can lead others to sunshine and safety with our positive example.

You can't control the words and actions of others. You won't be able to stop all the floodwaters that come your way. But you can wisely choose to use your own words and actions to keep the floodwaters at bay.

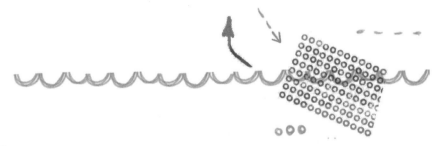

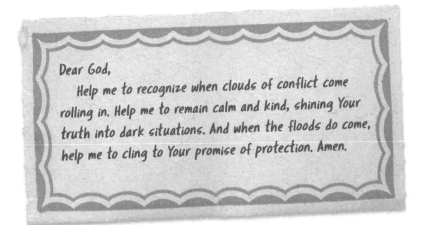

Dear God,
Help me to recognize when clouds of conflict come rolling in. Help me to remain calm and kind, shining Your truth into dark situations. And when the floods do come, help me to cling to Your promise of protection. Amen.

In the middle of the space below, draw a blue, flowing line from side to side. Below that line, in blue, write words or phrases that can cause a flood. Now above the line, in bright orange, write words of gentleness, kindness, and truth that can shine through the storm. Whenever you're faced with bad attitudes and unkind words, try to use those bright orange words to turn the tide of conflict.

SOLOMON SAYS: *Go back to page 56 to see what God thinks about stirring up trouble. Skip ahead to page 124 to see another way to stop anger in its tracks.*

58

A WISE LEGACY

A foolish son is grief to his father and bitterness to the one who bore him.—Proverbs 17:25

READ: PROVERBS 17:21-28

Has there ever been a time when you made your mom or dad really proud? I'm sure there has been! What was it that you did? And what did your parents do to show how much it meant to them?

On the other hand, has there ever been a time when you messed up really badly? If your parents were disappointed, what was their response? Hopefully it was still truthful and gracious.

We all mess up from time to time, but the encouraging news is that we have the chance to do better the next time. God is full of chances, especially when we aren't trying to do wrong to begin with. It's really important, though, to realize the impact that choices have on our parents and also on your future children. You might not think about it at your age, but every choice you make *now* will affect the type of parent you become *down the line*. If you spend time disobeying your parents, you might want to buckle up for a ride when you meet your firstborn someday!

Today's Scriptures share with us that foolishness makes parents sad and broken in spirit. But changing that situation can, instead, create a wise legacy. That means: *right choices now prepare you for a good outcome later.* Creating a wise legacy is like leaving a good path to follow. How you interpret the world around you now will help you when it's time to serve someone well later. The small things today can be the big things tomorrow!

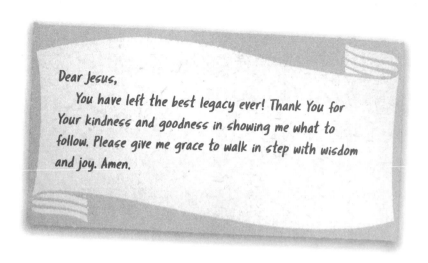

Dear Jesus,
    You have left the best legacy ever! Thank You for Your kindness and goodness in showing me what to follow. Please give me grace to walk in step with wisdom and joy. Amen.

Board game day! Choose a board game at your house that involves following a path (maybe The Game of Life, Monopoly, or even Mouse Trap!). Enjoy following its prompts to get to the end of the trail. When you get stuck or sent back a few spaces, take a minute to remind yourself that life is like that too. Take a deep breath, learn something new, and wait for your next turn. When you get ahead, celebrate that God gives us wisdom to plow ahead at times. Your board game might not perfectly represent your life, but it's a fun way to think about your future. Grab your parents and have them play too!

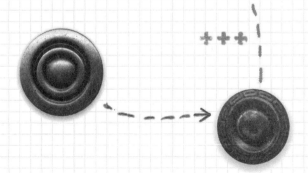

59

SELFLESS > SELFISH

One who isolates himself pursues selfish desires; he rebels against all sound wisdom. A fool does not delight in understanding, but only wants to show off his opinions.
—Proverbs 18:1–2

- - - → **READ: PROVERBS 18:1–4**

Read those verses again. Did anyone come to mind? I can think of a few examples. And sometimes, to be honest, it's *myself*.

Selfish behavior is pretty normal for a toddler. "My toy. My snack. Mine. Mine. Miiiine!" But at some point, we have to grow out of it. If we truly want to make room for strong relationships in our lives, we have to look beyond our own thoughts and opinions and desires. We have to move from toddler-like selfishness to more mature selflessness.

In these two verses, Solomon focuses on two major forms of selfishness. First up is our selfish desires or wants, which sounds like a grown-up thing. But think about it. When you get up in the morning, what are your goals, your desires? Are you thinking about Mom having a good morning? Are you wondering whether your sister found her chemistry folder? Or are you perfecting your hair in the mirror? (Don't answer that.)

Second is our selfish opinions. From toddlers to grown-ups, we *all* need work on this one. When someone disagrees with your opinion, do you immediately dismiss it? Or do you really listen? Do you "delight in understanding" their point of view? If not, well, Solomon has a certain word for that.

It only makes sense that when we focus on no one but ourselves, we "isolate" ourselves. We create a lonely world with narrow opinions formed by nothing but our own experience. But when we consider the concerns and goals of others, when we really listen and try to understand, we not only better ourselves, but we make the world a better place for everyone in it.

Dear Jesus,
    Forgive my selfish heart. As I go through each day, help me to notice and to listen to the needs and opinions of others. Help me to see them as You do and to listen and act as You would. In Your name I pray, amen.

Think about all of the people in your life, especially those you don't always agree with. What are their likes and dislikes? What are their needs and their wants? Does your brother like oatmeal raisin cookies, when clearly brownies are better? Does your sister always want to play your least favorite game? Does your mom really, *really* want you to eat the green stuff on your plate? Make a list of their names, and beside each name, write one nice thing you could do for them. Then go, and do that thing. Look for ways, every day, that you can act selflessly in love.

60

WOUNDING WORDS

A fool's lips lead to strife, and his mouth provokes a beating.
—Proverbs 18:6

READ: PROVERBS 18:5-8;
LUKE 6:45

Words have so much power. They can create joy or heartbreak.

Can you imagine if the words we spoke showed up on the T-shirts of the people we spoke to? What do you think your friends' shirts would say? Would they have encouraging, supportive, and helpful words on them? Or unnecessary, frustrated, or rude words on them?

Sometimes we have to pull ourselves back when we are in a situation where we might lose track of our words. As today's proverb says, words can wound and lead to strife, and they can also increase the chance to be wounded back. It's wise to keep those lips under control and choose when and where to let them speak.

Telling someone "no" quickly or speaking when you should be quiet might trigger the listener to respond with harshness or be offended. So when you're tempted to lose your cool or open your mouth, take a minute to stop. Is it the right time to speak? If so, then look the person you're speaking to in the eyes, take a deep breath, and reply with kindness and quietness. It can make a huge difference!

And if you realize you've said something you shouldn't have said, just stop.

Breathe.

Apologize.

And try again.

Or just stay quiet if that's the right choice. We're all trying, learning, and growing. Saying sorry when we've missed our opportunity opens the door to finishing well. It's never too late to do the right thing.

Dear Jesus,

Please guard my mouth! Put a zip over my lips when I need to be quiet, and give me grace to speak truth well when it's time to share. I want to use my words to encourage and not to wound. Amen.

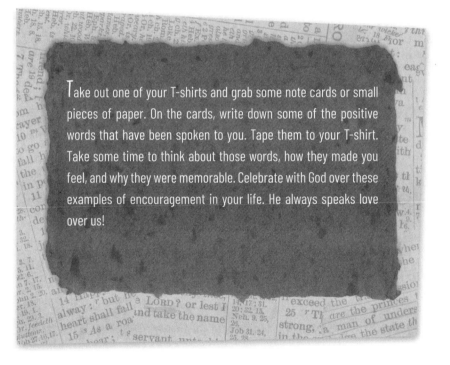

Take out one of your T-shirts and grab some note cards or small pieces of paper. On the cards, write down some of the positive words that have been spoken to you. Tape them to your T-shirt. Take some time to think about those words, how they made you feel, and why they were memorable. Celebrate with God over these examples of encouragement in your life. He always speaks love over us!

61

HUMILITY WINS

Before his downfall a person's heart is proud, but humility comes before honor.—Proverbs 18:12

READ: PROVERBS 18:9-21

Before opening this book, you'd probably heard the saying, "Pride goes before the fall." It's pulled straight from Proverbs! You might have also heard the Greek myth of Icarus, who made wings of wax. His pride led him to fly too close to the sun (wax wings + sun = not a good day for Icarus). In this world that seems to revolve around prestige, popularity, and perfection, we need a lot of warnings about the downfalls of pride.

If pride, as Solomon so clearly states, comes before a downfall, why do we let ourselves get so caught up in it? Would you willingly get on a train that you *knew* would run off the tracks? Probably not. I suspect the reason we *do* is that we just don't recognize our own pride until it's much too late.

And if humility, as Solomon says, leads to honor, why don't we practice that more often? Why are we not continually pointing to God as the source of all glory and honor? Why are we not always bending low to serve the needs of others? I suspect the same reason is true here too.

So, let's do something about it. Right now. Let's make a commitment to each other to win this game of life. Let's toss away all notions of prestige and popularity and perfection. Let's turn all the attention to God when our gifts and accomplishments are honored. Let's step down off the train that's heading nowhere and look around at those who could use a hand. Let's serve this world with humility and let God have all the honor.

Dear God,

I know I can get all caught up in myself sometimes. But I realize that this life is not all about me. It's all about You. Show me Your plan and Your purposes. And show me how to work in humility to serve You and Your people each and every day. Amen.

Think about some proud moments in your life. Either write them down or walk around your house and look at the trophies or photos that represent those moments. As you do, think about what God did to make all those moments possible. From the gifts and talents He's given you to the family and friends He's placed around you, God is responsible for every good and perfect gift (James 1:17). Thank Him in humility and give Him all the glory for the good things in your life.

_____

_____

_____

_____

_____

_____

SOLOMON SAYS: *Go back to page 108 to read more about the power of humility.*

FINDING A GOOD THING

A man who finds a wife finds a good thing and obtains favor from the LORD.—Proverbs 18:22

READ: PROVERBS 18:22-24

It might seem a bit odd to think about looking for a wife (or husband) at your current age. So weird, right? But at the same time, not-so-weird.

Though you may not be looking for a spouse right now (understandably), this time in your life is actually teaching you and giving you the freedom to find yourself in bigger ways, and that is something you will take with you well into your adulthood and possibly into (someday) a marriage. If most adults could go back to their younger years, there might be a few things they'd think through *then* that would have actually changed their *now*.

I know, I know. It's hard to think of things that seem so far away, but for the sake of a really great learning opportunity, let's look at what Solomon says about finding a spouse: it brings favor with the Lord.

Choosing a spouse who honors God in his or her heart and actions will bring God's blessing, protection, and joy. Your daily routine, home, children, and life will all include your spouse. That person should encourage you to worship Jesus, help you make Godly decisions, and be your most supportive companion. A future husband or wife should be someone you find wise, someone who is like-minded on important things like your faith, and someone you enjoy!

Finding a Godly spouse will make for a favorable life story then, won't it? Thank you, Proverbs!

Dear Jesus,
    Today I pray for wisdom in finding a good spouse someday if that's Your plan for me! Though marriage may seem really far away, it's never too early to talk to You about it. Help me to start now to value what You value in relationships. I look forward to seeing You work in my future! Amen.

It's list time! A good list is the sign of a thoughtful and intentional person; it can also help you focus on what God considers important for your life. Even though you're not getting married anytime soon, spend a few minutes thinking through some things you think God values in relationships and in choosing the right spouse. You might write down characteristics such as honesty, kindness, patience, wisdom, and a love for Jesus. This list simply gets your prayers moving and helps you focus on God's plans for you in the long run. Not only can you begin to look for and appreciate these characteristics in others, but you can check to see if you're developing the list in your own life.

8
9
10
11
12
13
14
15
16
17
18
19
20

63

WALK IT, TALK IT

Better a poor person who lives with integrity than someone who has deceitful lips and is a fool.—Proverbs 19:1

READ: PROVERBS 19:1-3

We've been hanging out with Solomon for sixty-three days now (if you're reading this devotional in order). And we're stepping into our nineteenth chapter of Proverbs. So what have you learned so far from the world's wisest king?

It is our hope that you're standing a little taller, speaking a little more wisely, and being a little kinder to those around you (not that you weren't *already* tall, wise, and kind). We want you to walk away from this devotional not only with more wisdom on the *inside* but also a new way of life on the *outside*.

In fact, if we were to sum up what Solomon is trying to pass along in these proverbs, in a word, it would probably be *integrity*. Integrity can be difficult to explain, but we know it when we see it, don't we? Someone we can trust. Someone who is respectful of others. Someone who speaks the truth. Someone who does the right thing—whether others are watching or not. When we continue to make wise choices, it builds a life of integrity.

On the flip side, Solomon shows us the other option: a fool. And we know what that looks like, too, don't we? Someone who's careless and dishonest. Someone who's always laughing at the expense of another. Someone causing trouble every time the teacher turns her back. Solomon warns us again and again not to be that person.

Solomon says it so simply (for those of us who *aren't* the world's wisest king). We can live a life of integrity, or we can live the life of a fool. We want you to take all that you've learned from Solomon and use it to shape your life. We want everyone to learn from your example, to look at *you* and say, "Now there is a person who lives with integrity!"

Dear God,

Thank You for sharing Your wisdom with us. Help me never to take it for granted. Help me to continue to learn and apply all that I've learned to my life, to my actions, and to my words. Help me build a life that honors You. Amen.

Write the letters of *integrity* in a vertical row below. From each letter, write a word (or phrase) starting with each of those letters that help to describe a person of integrity. If you need help, read back through some of Solomon's words, and see how he describes a life of integrity.

64

LOVE YOURSELF

The one who acquires good sense loves himself; one who safeguards understanding finds success. —Proverbs 19:8

READ: PROVERBS 19:4–10

Have you ever been on an airplane when the flight attendant goes over the rules for the oxygen masks? If you have, you know that he or she always reminds the passengers to put on their own masks before assisting someone else with theirs. Seems wise, doesn't it? You can't help someone else if you haven't helped yourself!

Sometimes this world is chaotic. So chaotic, in fact, that it's easy to get frazzled, exhausted, and worked up over things that could be more easily dealt with by wisdom! Scripture reminds us often that receiving knowledge and understanding is like creating a healthy boundary for ourselves. Understanding how to guard our decisions and our time gives us better opportunities for legitimate growth. When we understand wisdom, we care for ourselves well. This makes us able to care for others also.

So, stay wise and put your mask on first! When you are prepared in your life, you can be ready to use that wisdom to help the world around you.

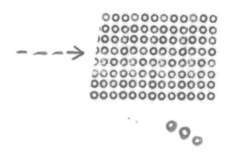

Dear God,
    Life can be complex, and it's easy to get caught up in doing a lot all the time. Help me to remember to grow my wisdom, to create healthy boundaries, and to rest in You. Thank You for teaching us to safeguard Your words so that we can care for ourselves and others well. Amen.

This may be the easiest activity you'll ever do! It's called: rest! Resting in God is like receiving oxygen when you need it most. Take fifteen to twenty minutes today to put away all electronics, music, noise, and busyness. Close your eyes, find a comfy spot on the couch, and take a few deep breaths. Then, simply allow yourself the joy of quietly recharging.

65

PATIENCE AND ANGER

A person's insight gives him patience, and his virtue
is to overlook an offense. A king's rage is like the
roaring of a lion, but his favor is like dew on the grass.
—Proverbs 19:11–12

READ: ROMANS 5:1–5

Think about a time when you messed up. Big time. How did the people around you respond? Would you categorize their response as patience? Or more like wrath? Which one would you prefer? When we're on the receiving end, it's safe to say that we'd all prefer patience over wrath.

What about when others upset *you*? When *they* mess up big time? How do you respond? Are you more like the king's roar or his morning dew?

Solomon says that patience is a result of insight, meaning good sense or wisdom. So once again we see the importance of wisdom. It helps us pause and consider the feelings and circumstances of others before we react. In doing so, we not only avoid losing our cool and hurting others, but we also prevent the guilt that would follow before it even starts.

Another translation of this verse says that it's our "glory to overlook an offense" (ESV). So patience goes much, much farther than that moment in time. Regularly practicing patience—even when we don't want to, even when it's hard—will help us to grow in character, will reflect God, and will shine down rays of hope on what could be a dark or difficult situation.

Bad things are going to happen. People are going to mess up. And we can either respond with patience or with anger and rage. But always remember that how we respond matters. Our response not only affects those around us, but it also says a lot about who we are.

Dear God,

I'm sorry for every time I've messed up. Thank You for responding to me in patience and not with anger. Help me to respond to others in the same way, always ready to overlook their offenses, offering them the gift of patience, just as You have given to me. Amen.

Take another look at Proverbs 19:12, noticing the imagery Solomon chose for patience and rage, the "dew on the grass" and the "roaring of a lion." Think of other images you could use to represent patience and anger. Maybe they're both animals, scenes from nature, or fictional characters. Whatever they are, sketch, color, and bring them to life on paper, creating visual images of the choices you have when responding to difficult situations every day.

GOD'S PLAN WINS

Many plans are in a person's heart, but the LORD's decree will prevail.—Proverbs 19:21

READ: PROVERBS 19:13–29

It's very common to have a plan for your day. What would life be like if no one had a schedule or had to be at work or school on time? It would seem hectic or chaotic, wouldn't it? A plan is a good idea so that our lives have some organization and order. It's smart to have an idea of what you're doing or where you're going. That is wisdom!

However . . .

More important than *our* plans and schedules, God has all His plans for us each day and even for our whole lives! He knows what He wants for us and what is best for us, and He also knows the prayers we will pray and the choices we will make. So before we start putting plans into action, it's always wise to read our Bibles, pray, and ask God what *His plan* is first. Our days and lives will run more smoothly because we are agreeing with His will instead of making our own. Smart, right?

It's no fun to make a big plan only to realize after a bunch of hard work that God never intended that plan for you. It's actually quite frustrating! God can always stop our plan to correct us and make room for His. It's not because He is mad at us; it's because He knows what is best for us.

So, the next time you have a big dream you want to follow or an idea to create, take some time to pray about it until you get a sense for where God is inside it. God always speaks to us when we choose to rest in Him, and His plan is always a winner.

Dear God,

Your plans are always best. I will follow You! Thank You for designing the best plans for me even when I might not be able to see them right away. Help me always to pray first, plan afterward, and act when You say so. Amen.

Take out a piece of paper and fold it into a small origami figure. You can fold the layers any way you like and create any shape. After crafting your piece, hand it to a family member with a simple assignment: Copy this design, and make three identical shapes.

What do you think your family member will do? Figure out the design by scratch or ask you for instructions? It makes sense that she will ask you how you made it and then make three copies from there, doesn't it? Having God's instructions are just like that. He creates a great plan, and we can follow it to succeed. See how your family member responds, and then make a few copies together to give to friends.

SOW HONOR

A righteous person acts with integrity; his children who come after him will be happy.—Proverbs 20:7

READ: PROVERBS 20:1-9

Have you ever thought about the seeds you're planting or sowing each day? Are they seeds of kindness and love? Bitterness and anger? Or seeds of indifference, like you don't even care?

Those seeds that you're planting will soon take root and grow up tall where everyone can see them. They could stretch out tall and wide like an apple tree, with plenty of fruit to go around. They could be tough and unruly weeds that cause problems wherever they grow. Or they could just smell terrible like the corpse flower. (It's a real thing.) Jesus teaches us that we will know who people are by the fruit they bear (Matthew 7:20). The kind of fruit you bear tomorrow depends entirely on the seeds you're planting today.

When you're too young to have the wisdom of Solomon, you don't think too much about the seeds you're planting. You don't think too much about how a mean word will dig deep and fester or how that kind gesture will grow and bloom. But now you have the wisdom of Solomon. And now you know.

In this same chapter, Solomon says, "The slacker does not plow during planting season; at harvest time he looks, and there is nothing" (Proverbs 20:4). But we're not slackers, are we? We are plowing and sowing all the seeds. They may be tiny seeds, but just you wait. Those nice words, those helpful acts, those quiet prayers—they're all seeds that will grow into trees that will bloom and bear beautiful, nurturing fruit. With the good seeds you're planting today, you will allow others to share in the harvest of goodness and kindness and love.

Sow those seeds wisely, my friends.

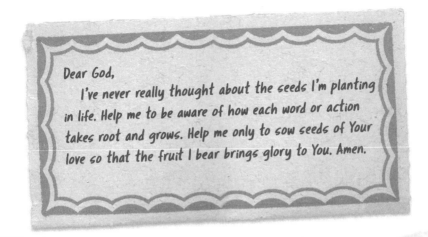

Dear God,
    I've never really thought about the seeds I'm planting in life. Help me to be aware of how each word or action takes root and grows. Help me only to sow seeds of Your love so that the fruit I bear brings glory to You. Amen.

Think for a minute about the different kinds of seeds that you can sow, like kind words, good deeds, or even selfishness or anger. Now, draw a brown line across the empty space below. Under the brown line, draw the different seeds in a row. Draw their roots shooting out, and color in the dirt around them. Now above the dirt line, draw plants to represent what you're growing. Show them fully grown with the fruit they will bear. Put a little plant marker beside each that labels the types of seeds that were sown, the type of plants that will grow. Let your garden remind you of the fruit you will bear when you sow good seeds.

SOLOMON SAYS: Go back to page 78 for more about growing deep roots.

68

KNOWN BY YOUR ACTIONS

Even a young man is known by his actions—by whether his behavior is pure and upright.—Proverbs 20:11

READ: PROVERBS 20:10-21; 1 TIMOTHY 4:12

If you're reading this book about our friend Solomon and his wise words, chances are you're what some may call a tween or teen. Others may call you a young person, and some might still say kid. Just because your age might not fit you into the cuddly baby stage or the independent, college-age category, you have so much to contribute to this world!

That's why this devotional was hand-chosen for you. The decisions you make now are already showing who you are and shaping your future. It's a gift to be able to learn these lessons at an early age because your life will be formed by the wisdom and integrity you build now. Even though you are young, your life is already influential. Think about it. . . . Offering friendship to the "unpopular" kid at school. Not yelling angry words when the other goalie cheats in the big game. Leaving your friend's house when the guys choose to play the wrong kind of video game. Each action shapes what you are becoming and how you are known.

Choosing to be faithful and pure will have positive, long-lasting repercussions, not only on you but also on the other people who are lucky enough to learn from you. Remember, Solomon was once your age, and look where he ended up! Young or old, be glad to be known by your actions and your wisdom.

Dear God,

Thank You for teaching me Your ways, especially early in life. I'm grateful for the time, people, and resources that give me more opportunities to grow in You. Help me to stay hungry for Your Word and to live life with purity and uprightness. Amen.

Today is a day for Random Acts of Kindness! What you need to do is simple: find a few ways to give to others in ways that exemplify what you're learning through this book. Perhaps generously give your younger brother or sister a dollar to buy a treat, or sweep the kitchen floor without being asked. You could also take out the trash or thank your parents for all they do. No matter what you choose, you'll make your family smile, and you will be a great example to anyone who sees you!

✦ ✦ ✦ ✦ ✦ ✦

69

WAIT FOR GOD'S JUSTICE

Don't say, "I will avenge this evil!" Wait on the LORD, and he will rescue you.—Proverbs 20:22

READ: EXODUS 14

"**C**an you believe she just did that?! I'm gonna do the exact same thing to her! I'm gonna march right in there and . . ."

Whoaaa, there.

Solomon knows that people are going to do mean and hurtful things. They're going to hurt your feelings and break your stuff and say not-nice things about you. They're going to do things that you're never, ever going to want to forgive. And they are going to make. you. *mad.*

But in this proverb, Solomon is trying to get in front of the situation and give you a little advice: leave it up to God.

I know that's the biblical answer and we should believe it. But I also know that it's sometimes difficult to grasp the here-and-now reality of God. Will God *actually* serve justice to the people who have wronged you, to the people who wrong others? He will. I've seen it.

Moses and all God's people saw it when the armies of Egypt were chasing after them. "They were terrified and cried out to the LORD" (Exodus 14:10 NIV). And do you know what Moses said to them? "The LORD will fight for you; you need only to be still" (v. 14). And boy did He ever. (Just read the rest of Exodus 14 and see!)

God is the only one with enough wisdom to know what justice should look like. He's the only one who sees every detail of both sides of the situation. And He's the only one powerful enough to give true justice—punishment or reward—where it is due.

This is going to take patience. And it's going to take self-control. But this is the wisest way. Leave justice up to the Lord.

Dear God,

Please be with those who have wronged me. Whatever they're going through, whatever is going on in their lives and homes to make them act out in anger or bitterness, help them through those things. Help me to forgive those who wrong me and to leave justice up to You. Amen.

Take some time to read one (or a few!) stories of God's wise justice in the Bible. You could read the story of Joseph (Genesis 37–45), Moses (Exodus 14), or Jonah *after* the big fish (Jonah 3–4), to name a few. These are all examples of God interacting with the world to correct or protect His people. When you're finished, write or draw the words of Proverbs 20:22: "Wait on the Lord, and he will rescue you." And know that it is *true*.

70

COURAGE AND CLARITY

Even a courageous person's steps are determined by the LORD, so how can anyone understand his own way?—Proverbs 20:24

READ: PROVERBS 20:23-29; JOSHUA 1:9

Throughout Scripture, we often find verses about choosing courage and having no fear. And we're continually told that courage is possible because "the LORD" walks with us through the stressful spaces in life. Have you ever wondered why Scripture says *LORD* here and *God* or other names elsewhere? Why does God have so many names? Well, each name represents a different portion of who God is. The Bible is full of different examples of how God shows us Himself within His different names.

In the Scriptures for today's reading, God is called *LORD*. In the Bible, when LORD is written in small caps like this, it is using God's personal name and giving Him great respect, honor, and worship. It was the name God used when calling Himself "I AM." Let it be a reminder to you that God is all things . . . all-seeing and all-knowing and all-powerful. And He is the one determining our steps!

Isn't it nice to know that God has everything worked out in your life? Whether good or bad, everything has a purpose and can be used to make you better and stronger! You have room to feel a bit more brave, to try something new, or to be obedient even when it seems difficult. Reading the Bible can give us more understanding of what God might ask of us because He lays out all the instructions there, and He tells us His names. That's where we know He orders our steps for us. So in all good things, be courageous, because the LORD is on your side!

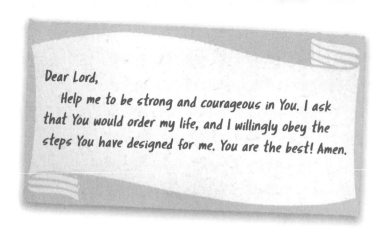

Dear Lord,

Help me to be strong and courageous in You. I ask that You would order my life, and I willingly obey the steps You have designed for me. You are the best! Amen.

Write down some things you might be a bit scared of. We all have a few! It could be spiders or taking tests or gym class at school. Write out Joshua 1:9 on a piece of paper (or even on your hand) until it's memorized deep into every little nook and cranny in your brain. Speak it out loud, and then keep showing up, even when you're nervous. God will be with you!

71

GOD KNOWS THE HEART

All a person's ways seem right to him, but the LORD weighs hearts.—Proverbs 21:2

READ: PROVERBS 21:1-3

How much does your heart weigh? Well, the average human heart weighs about ten ounces.* And it's about the size of a clenched fist. But my guess is that's not exactly what Solomon is talking about in this proverb.

If God were to weigh your heart, what would He get? (Besides about ten ounces.) Would it be heavy with grief or anger? Would it be full of bitterness and hatefulness? Or would it be light with joy and love?

The truth is, we probably have a little mixture of all the above—and more—depending on the given day. When you've won the game or made straight As or spent the day with your best friend, the heart, of course, is joyful. But on gray days when bad news comes, it tends to weigh on even the lightest hearts.

And God sees it all. He knows. He even knows, as Solomon says, when it seems like we're doing the right thing, but deep down, our hearts are in the wrong place. He knows when we're doing the wrong thing with good intentions. He knows it all. He weighs our hearts.

So what does this mean for us? Well, maybe we should spend a little time weighing our own hearts. Maybe we should pray the Psalm 139 prayer: "Search me, God, and know my heart; test me and know my concerns. See if there is any offensive way in me; lead me in the everlasting way" (vv. 23-24). When we do, we can be sure that when God puts our hearts on the scale, He is pleased with what He sees.

---

* https://www.livescience.com/34655-human-heart.html

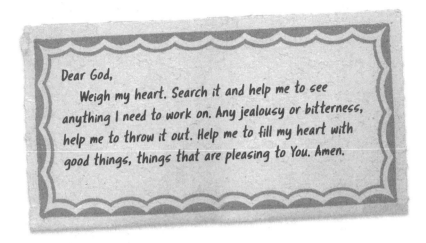

Dear God,

Weigh my heart. Search it and help me to see anything I need to work on. Any jealousy or bitterness, help me to throw it out. Help me to fill my heart with good things, things that are pleasing to You. Amen.

Find a ruler and some coins. Sort the coins by size and weight. Now, think of them as the various thoughts and emotions weighing on your heart. Holding the ruler in the center, place "good" coins, weights, emotions on one end of the ruler. Place "bad" thoughts and emotions on the other end. When you're finished, does your "scale" tip toward the good or bad end?

Of course, this isn't a test to see whether your heart is "good" or "bad." But it is most definitely an exercise to get you thinking about what's in your heart. Talk to God about what you've found, and ask for His help in keeping a healthy heart.

SOLOMON SAYS: Look back at page 110 for more on keeping a healthy heart.

72

DILIGENCE ROCKS!

The plans of the diligent certainly lead to profit, but anyone who is reckless certainly becomes poor.
—Proverbs 21:5

READ: PROVERBS 21:4-8

Have you ever saved for a long time to buy something you really wanted? If so, how did it feel? Most likely, it felt really satisfying because you worked hard, saw your savings slowly grow, and were finally able to get what you worked for. If you haven't had this experience, can you think of something you would like to start saving for?

Saving will take some diligence! *Diligence* is a word that means doing work carefully and without quitting. It means that every small step counts, and when you keep working, you'll keep growing. Solomon shares with us that diligence leads to profit or, in other words, more growth or extra gains! Unfortunately, if you're not so diligent, it can lead to becoming poor or not having enough of what you really need. You might end up spending all the money you needed for healthy food on things like sugary sweets. It could lead to a stomachache instead of energy to play.

What are some things in your life that you'd like to be diligent in working toward? Are they things you need or things you would like? What are some choices you've made recklessly, or without careful actions, that bummed you out as a result? These bad choices are helpful to think through so you can make a wiser plan the next time.

Think through these choices and plans, and you'll be sure to rock your way to success!

Dear Jesus,

Thank You for living a perfect example of a diligent life! Help me to be diligent in mine. I want to honor You with my small wins and big wins. Thank You for helping me learn how to succeed! Amen.

Today's the day to start saving for something. If you already have a piggy bank filling up, great! You can either add to it or start a new one for something specific. Ask your parents if you can earn money from a few extra chores and start adding to your bank. Perhaps you want to buy something you need or buy something you'd like, or maybe you even want to donate your earnings to a special cause at church or in your community. No matter which way you work, keep doing the small chores with big love, and you'll have accomplished quite a bit of profit for a purpose.

73

DON'T DO DRAMA

Better to live on the corner of a roof than to share a house with a nagging wife.—Proverbs 21:9

READ: PROVERBS 21:9-12, 19

I'm going to go out on a limb and guess that you're not married yet. But this proverb always makes me laugh. Can't you just picture a guy hanging out on the corner of his roof, hiding from a nagging wife? While the picture is pretty funny, there's a wise element of truth in this verse. And it's the first of a few proverbs in this passage that deal with dodging drama.

First, let's be clear. Emotions are good. They are natural indicators of how we feel and how we are affected by the circumstances around us. Crying is not always being dramatic. Being upset or angry is not, in itself, stirring up drama. But using those emotions to create controversy or to draw attention to yourself or to control other people is not a healthy practice.

More than likely, you've seen these kinds of drama in action. And in the passage above (Proverbs 21:9-12, 19), Solomon shares a few more examples: mocking others, desiring evil, not considering your neighbor, being hot-tempered, and of course, nagging. All these are unhealthy behaviors that can create drama.

Whether you're the one stirring it up or you just find yourself in the middle of a stirred-up situation, listen to what Solomon says and just *don't*. Don't do drama.

Instead, let's do the *opposite* of drama. Instead of making fun and being inconsiderate and nagging, let's share compliments and compassion and encouragement. Instead of stirring up negative emotions, let's seek out positive ones. Because as Jesus quite simply said, "Blessed are the peacemakers, for they will be called sons of God" (Matthew 5:9).

Dear God,
I know sometimes I get all caught up in my emotions and do or say things I don't mean. Forgive me for that. From this point on, help me to consider my emotions, what they mean, and how they affect those around me. Help me to bring my anger, my sadness, my frustration to You instead of using it against others. Help me to be a peacemaker, so that I can be called Your child. Amen.

Think of all the ways you can be a peacemaker today. Maybe you can write a note apologizing for something you did or said. Maybe you can make a card or a funny video for someone who is feeling bad. Maybe you can invite the "bully" to sit at your lunch table. Talk to God about how you can be a peacemaker. And whatever the two of you decide, GO and do that thing today.

74

GIVE RIGHT!

Justice executed is a joy to the righteous but a terror to evildoers.—Proverbs 21:15

READ: PROVERBS 21:13-16

What feels better than a wrong made right? It can be so frustrating if a sibling is rude to you, sets you up for trouble, or maybe even takes something from you without being asked. How about if a friend does it? It hurts, right? We often want people to have consequences when they do bad things. We want justice.

But what about when someone is punished for doing something wrong that you have done too? Are you happy that there was justice, or are you scared that you are going to have the same consequences? Justice can be hard to look at or think about if there's something in our hearts that God might not approve of. *Eek!* That's why David, Solomon's father, said to God in Psalm 51:10, "Create a clean heart for me and renew a steadfast spirit within me."

Solomon (and his dad) remind us that justice is joy! That means, if we are free in our hearts toward God and others, then we will want justice. We will be able to stand up for what is true and right, even when it is difficult.

We have nothing to fear when we know that we live in the center of who Jesus is, and He is justice.

JUSTICE

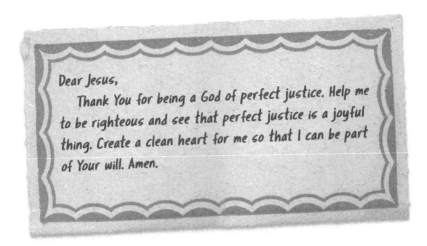

Dear Jesus,
   Thank You for being a God of perfect justice. Help me to be righteous and see that perfect justice is a joyful thing. Create a clean heart for me so that I can be part of Your will. Amen.

Order in the court! Let's choose one topic that needs justice in our world today. Your job is to take that case to court, write down why it is wrong, sit for a few minutes, and pray to God for it to change (ahem . . . ask Him how it might change inside your heart first). Then go out and do a small thing to make the world better. Being a world changer starts from David's simple prayer; you can be a world changer too!

_____

_____

_____

_____

_____

_____

SOLOMON SAYS: Go back to page 142 to read more about God's justice.

75

GOODNESS OVER PLEASURE

The one who loves pleasure will become poor. . . . The one who pursues righteousness and faithful love will find life, righteousness, and honor.—Proverbs 21:17, 21

READ: PROVERBS 21:17-22

Have you ever stepped back and thought about what you're pursuing in life? I know it's a big question. But it's a good idea, no matter what age or stage of life that you're in, to fly the drone up and get an aerial view from time to time.

When you think about the choices you've made in the last week or month or year, what has been the main goal? You can probably fit those goals into one of two categories: goodness or pleasure. Has it been all about you? About your comfort? About having fun? Or has it been about growing? About helping others? About just becoming a better person?

Of course, it's important to have a good laugh and to rest our bodies and minds. But Solomon is reminding us in these two verses that a life revolving around our own pleasure is a wasteful life. We miss our God-given purposes when we live our lives to please only ourselves.

Solomon also shows us the other side, the life pursuit with a big payoff. Very simply, he says, "The one who pursues righteousness and faithful love will find life, righteousness, and honor." What would that look like for you? For your whole life? How can you make today and every day about pursuing goodness and love?

> Dear God,
>   I know sometimes I make things all about myself. Forgive me for that. Help me to look beyond myself to see Your purposes for my life. Help me to grow in goodness and love so that I may reflect You more and more every day. Amen.

Do you remember your goals from page 107? How are you doing on them? Considering those goals and your progress, let's create a revised goal list. Think about what you've accomplished and what you still need to work on. Create a list with a daily goal, a monthly goal, and a yearly goal. And be sure that those goals work with your pursuit of "righteousness and faithful love." Check in from time to keep yourself on track so that one day you will "find life, righteousness, and honor."

_____

_____

_____

_____

_____

_____

_____

_____

_____

_____

_____

_____

SOLOMON SAYS: Go back to page 62 for more on our life pursuits.

76

LISTENING BEATS LYING

A lying witness will perish, but the one who listens will speak successfully.—Proverbs 21:28

> READ: PROVERBS 21:23–31

It's no good to be caught in a lie. It can be embarrassing, sad, and harmful to a person's reputation. Sometimes people lie because they get scared, they fear being in trouble, or maybe they know they did wrong and don't want to get caught. There are many reasons why kids, and even adults, choose to be dishonest instead of facing up to the truth.

Honesty can feel vulnerable at first, like it exposes something about us that we might not want to face. But honesty also produces courage because it gives people a chance to do what is right, even if it's difficult. Have you ever had a chance to be brave by telling the truth instead of covering something up with a lie?

Solomon talked about lying previously in his writings (remember Proverbs 6:16 on page 56?) as one of the things God hates. *Hate* is such a strong word, yet Solomon uses it to describe how God feels about lying. That means it's pretty serious.

Solomon also goes on to say in today's proverb that "one who listens will speak successfully." Let's take that as advice to slow down, listen before speaking too quickly, and watch the words and actions that come from our mouths and hearts. Better to be slow and successful than rushed and caught in a lie that God hates!

> Dear God,
>   Please help me to slow down in my actions so that I can make healthy choices. Please also help me to listen carefully, choose my words wisely, and be truthful in what I say and do. Give me courage to stand in the middle of difficult situations. Thank You for being with me! Amen.

Older family members can help with today's activity! Ask them to write down four different Bible verses. Then ask them to write down a few quotes by famous people and a few quotes or statements that are totally made up and false. Finish by asking your family member to read the notes one at a time in a random order. Listen carefully as they read. Then guess if each quote or note is actually in the Bible or potentially a lie! Were you right? This activity is a good reminder of the importance of listening well and how tricky lies can be.

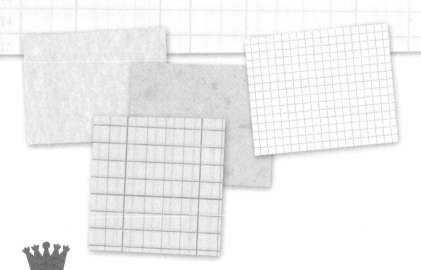

SOLOMON SAYS: Go back to page 56 to see the seven things God hates.

77

SEEING THROUGH GOD'S EYES

Rich and poor have this in common: the LORD makes them all.
—Proverbs 22:2

READ: PROVERBS 22:1-9

Have you ever seen a person on the street asking for money? Or a video about a hungry child on TV? What did you do when you saw them? Look away? Change the channel? Say a prayer?

Sometimes it's difficult to know just how to react when we see people having a hard time. But Solomon gives us these wise words: "The LORD makes them all." The scraggly guy on the side of the road? God dreamed him up. The little one crying on TV? A miracle from God Himself. The woman in jail, the college kid living in a van, the classmate in need of a bath—God made them and *loves them all*.

Sure, this world isn't how God created it to be. He gave the first humans a beautiful garden full of everything they would ever need, flowers of every color, fruits and veggies of every shape and size. God's garden was abundant in every way. But Adam and Eve, the first humans, thought they could do better. They chose their way over God's way. And ever since then, the world has been cursed, out of balance. Instead of everyone having enough, some people have too much, and other people go hungry. No matter how we try, humans have not been able to recreate the provision and abundance of God's perfect garden.

As a result, to this day, we see people with greed and need, hatefulness and hunger, excess and emptiness. But regardless of their circumstances, God made them all. God made *us* all.

So when you see someone different from you, someone struggling, someone looking down at you, someone sad or lonely or poor, remember who made them. Remember who loves them. And remember who has been called to love them too. (That's you.)

○○ ○○○ ○○○ ○○○ ○○○

Dear God,

Open my eyes to the people around me, the people You made, the people You love. Show me how to help them, how to pray for them every day. Help me to look them in the eyes and show them what I know: that You made them and You love them so. Amen.

Find John 13:34 in your Bible. Read those words, and then write them out (or just a portion of them) below and on a piece of paper. Doodle around them. Color them. And hang them where you will always remember to love God's people—all of them.

BFF

The one who loves a pure heart and gracious lips—the king is his friend.—Proverbs 22:11

READ: PROVERBS 22:10-14; MATTHEW 5:8

Who wouldn't want to be BFF with the king? And even better, *the King of kings*? Matthew 5:8 shares that "blessed are the pure in heart, for they will see God." Today's verse in Proverbs adds to it by saying: "The one who loves a pure heart and gracious lips—the king is his friend."

So, if you start with a pure heart, you have two advantages: you see God! Whoa—what can be cooler than that? Then, if you add some gracious speech, you also get to be His friend.

Though it might seem like you can make an *amigo* anywhere—at school, the park, sports practice, or any other place—how amazing is it that you can also be chosen as God's friend? You have been picked to be pals with the Creator of the universe! That means that no matter what happens—good or bad, wrong or right, whether you're struggling or succeeding—you are not alone.

In a day and age when "friends" can be simplified to likes on a screen, you can be safe and secure in the fact that you are chosen to be a comrade to the King. The man who came to die to make all wrong things right, to secure a relationship with us, and to live inside our hearts, wants to be your best friend—Jesus!

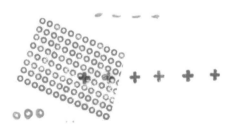

Dear Jesus,

Thank You for inviting me to be Your friend! Help me to choose gracious words as I learn how to better walk with You and live for You. I'm grateful that the King of kings is so invested in me. Amen.

What are some of the things you like to do with your closest friends? I bet you can do some of those with God as well. Set aside a half hour to do a few small activities with God by your side. You can talk to Him (out loud even!), meet Him for a smoothie, practice soccer with Him, or anything you like. Enjoy being with the One who loves you and calls you His friend.

✦ ✦ ✦ ✦ ✦ ✦

APPLY YOUR HEART

Pay attention and turn your ear to the sayings of the wise; apply your heart to what I teach, for it is pleasing when you keep them in your heart and have all of them ready on your lips.—Proverbs 22:17-18 NIV

READ: PROVERBS 22:15-19

You know how to apply your brain to a science test. You do your homework, you study, and you memorize terms.

You know how to apply your physical strength to a soccer game. You exercise, you practice, and you give your all on the field.

But for these "sayings of the wise," these proverbs, Solomon is asking you to "apply your heart." How exactly are you supposed to do that?

Well, maybe you already are. Reading this book (come on, you've made it to the seventy-ninth entry in this thing!) already has you thinking pretty regularly about wisdom. And I'm hoping by now you've put some of these wise sayings to work. And maybe, just maybe, you've even seen some hearts changed—your own heart, for starters—as a result.

When you take that first step by actually opening a book or your Bible to seek Godly wisdom, you begin to apply your heart. When you say a prayer, asking God for insight or help, you are applying your heart. And when you step out in the world around you, reach out to the people you love, and use this wisdom to make the world a better place, you are most definitely applying your heart.

Just like your brain and your strength, when you apply your heart to these wise sayings, your heart changes. It grows stronger. It becomes more joyful. And as Solomon says, it results in a life more pleasing to you, more pleasing in the eyes of God.

Dear God,

Help me always to hunger for Your teaching, Your wisdom. Help me apply my heart to Your words. Help me always to value Your words and Your wisdom, because above all, they lead to a truly pleasing and purposeful life. Amen.

Sketch a large heart below. Inside the heart, write some of the "sayings of the wise" you have learned, some of the sayings to which you have applied your heart. Think of how you have put these sayings to work and how they have made your life more pleasing to yourself and more pleasing to God.

GOD PROTECTS THE POOR

Don't rob a person because he is poor, and don't crush the oppressed at the city gate, for the LORD will champion their cause and will plunder those who plunder them.
—Proverbs 22:22-23

- - - → **READ: PROVERBS 22:20-23; PSALM 82:3-4**

Have you ever heard of the term *underdog*? It usually refers to someone who is expected not to win or overcome something. An underdog is often the last one chosen or the least loved. Sometimes, a person who is poor is considered an underdog because in our world most people expect money to win. But while Jesus was on earth, He spent most of His time with people who were poor. He knew they were valuable and worthy of His time! He wasn't afraid of the poor, nor did He speak down to them or crush them with His actions.

We, too, have the opportunity to serve the poor while we walk on this earth. Maybe it could be bringing dinner to those who need something to eat, collecting blankets or scarves through the winter to give to those who are cold, or donating to a church or organization that serves those in need in our area. We can help in so many ways! And even more than that, learning more about and showing respect to those who are poor is a thoughtful, loving, and honoring way to care. When we learn the stories of those who live or have lived in poor conditions, we learn compassion and understanding instead of judgment. We have the opportunity to love and support someone who may never have been supported.

So the next time you see someone in need, remind yourself to extend love and a prayer to bless them. Because just as those in poverty are often considered the underdog, so was Jesus! Although people expected Him to be born to royalty, He was instead born to young parents who were poor and kind, yet He saved the world.

Dear Jesus,

Thank You for coming to earth as a poor baby. Thank You for the love and life You show to those who have less than others. Help me to honor and help those who are in need and to never oppress anyone I think I have power over. Amen.

Let's get practical! What is one way you can give to the needy in your area today? Ask your parents if there is a food bank where you can donate canned goods. Or ask if there is an extra chore you can do to save a little money to give to an organization that is helping those in need. A little bit goes a long way! And if you get the chance, ask those who work at that organization a few questions about the work they do and the people they serve. Learn how to care for others well!

81

AVOID ANGER

Don't make friends with an angry person, and don't be a companion of a hot-tempered one, or you will learn his ways and entangle yourself in a snare.—Proverbs 22:24-25

READ: PROVERBS 22:24-29

Raise your hand if you know someone with a hot temper. Someone who seems to be angry and complains all the time. Someone you tiptoe around so that you don't accidentally step on their toes.

It seems that Solomon knew someone like that too. And he advises us to steer clear.

Whether we like it or not, whether we intend it or not, we pick up on the behavior of those around us. We start to say the same sayings and do the same things as the people we hang around. And for these reasons, Solomon says pretty plainly "don't make friends" with people like this.

That sounds kind of harsh, but in Solomon's wisdom, he knows. He knows how being around angry people will affect your behavior. He knows that you'll begin to think angry outlashes are normal and okay. He knows that it will cause you to develop unhealthy behaviors of your own.

These angry, hot-tempered people will make excuses like, "Well, that's just the way I am." Or "I can't help it if so-and-so makes me mad." But that's just not true. We've learned in this book that we *can* take control of our emotions. We can replace our angry thoughts with good thoughts. We can respond in patience instead of wrath.

And although Solomon advises against getting close with angry people, you can still love them. You can be an example for them, showing them the right way to respond to difficult situations. You can listen to them when they're upset. But now that you have Solomon's wisdom, you know better than to respond in anger, than to "entangle yourself" in the snare—the trap—of anger.

Dear God,
Forgive me for the times when I've lashed out in anger. Help me to be a good example of how to respond in difficult situations. Help me to guide those around me who are dealing with bad days and big emotions. Help me to respond to them in patience and to love them like You do. Amen.

When anger comes, it often strikes unexpectedly, burning everyone in its path. So, just as you would make a fire escape plan, let's make a plan to avoid anger. Read back through this devotional, especially pages 118 and 134 and any others you think might help. Write or draw out your escape plan for whenever a hot-tempered person burns out of control. Then study your plan so that when the unexpected strikes, you will be ready to respond calmly and avoid the consuming fire of anger.

SOLOMON SAYS: *Go back to pages 118 and 134 for other ways to avoid anger.*

82

GET RICH?

Don't wear yourself out to get rich; because you know better, stop! As soon as your eyes fly to it, it disappears, for it makes wings for itself and flies like an eagle to the sky.—Proverbs 23:4-5

READ: PROVERBS 23:1-8

It can be really tough to get rich. And even if you do, it often leaves as quickly as it comes. It can be easy to think that a lot of money will make troubles go away, but being able to buy anything you want can actually make your life worse!

Have you ever received money for your birthday? Maybe it started burning a hole in your pocket, and you felt like you had to spend it. If you already knew what you wanted to buy, the result might have been fine. But if you didn't know what you wanted, you might have gone to the store too quickly and bought something you really didn't need or like. And once the money was gone, you were likely looking at the next thing you wanted to buy.

The same thing happens when you work hard for the sake of getting rich. You might say you want to spend most of your time doing chores so that you can get a lot of money to spend. *(There's a chance, right?)* But if you're only working for the money, it is a waste. The money will just disappear, and you'll be left with nothing.

What might you miss out on when you are working so hard to get extra money? You might miss out on the people right in front of you who want to spend time with you, or you might get frustrated with others because you're so focused on making more money. "More, more, more" can actually turn into "frustrated, rushed, and angry" because your goal is always flying away from you.

Working hard is not a bad thing (not at all!). But it's important to think through what is really worth your time and energy and the purposes behind what you do. If you wear yourself out trying to get rich, remember to stop, because you know better! Look at your life, and see if all the details line up with what God says is right.

Dear Lord,

You are bigger than money. Your presence is worth more to me than riches. I want to listen to Your wisdom about how to slow down and work hard for You rather than for money. Thank You for teaching me the way of life! Amen.

What are some things you want to be known for? Take the time today to write those things down. If someone says your name, what do you want people to think of? Would it be that you were always trying to get more, were always busy, and were never around, or would it be that you loved well, lived well, worked hard, and also focused on the beautiful things in life? Make choices for your day that help create the life you want to live.

83

CORRECTION SAVES A LIFE

Do not withhold discipline from a child; if you punish them with the rod, they will not die. Punish them with the rod and save them from death.—Proverbs 23:13-14 NIV

READ: PROVERBS 23:9-18

I'm just going to come out and say it: the Bible can seem harsh sometimes. It was written centuries ago when societies and certainly parenting practices were much different. Slaves were acceptable workers, for starters, and apparently parents used rods to discipline their children.

But one thing remains the same, no matter how much time passes: God's Word is truth. And if we're being honest, well, sometimes we need things to be said bluntly.

I'm happy to say that I've never been punished with a rod—whatever that means. But I'm also happy to say that I understand the truth in this message. Correction is good for us. Without correction, we'd never know that we were going the wrong way.

If you're riding down a road and the bridge is out ahead, don't you *want* someone to tell you the bridge is out? Yeah, me too. And that is where correction, however painful or inconvenient, comes in handy. It can quite literally save a life.

When we're making wrong decisions, when we're being hateful or rude, when we're on a path that is leading nowhere but the bottom of a cliff, someone needs to step in. Someone wise. But regardless of how harsh it may seem, sometimes we need correction to save our lives.

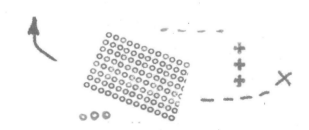

Dear God,

Thank You for putting people in my life to guide and correct me, to show me when I'm going the wrong way. Help me to be respectful and grateful for those people. And help me to use their correction to change directions. Amen.

Let's think about correction for a minute. Let's think about the kinds of discipline that work (and don't). Make a list of any discipline you've received from parents, teachers, or coaches, along with what you did wrong that needed correction. What was the result? Did the discipline correct the behavior? If not, what do you think would have? Getting disciplined is no fun. But I assure you, being the one to give discipline is no fun either. Thank your parents for being there to lead and guide you, and maybe even talk to them about different ideas for discipline that you think would serve you well and even save your life.

SOLOMON SAYS: Go back to page 30 for more on our favorite topic: correction!

84

PITFALLS OF PARTYING

Listen, my son, and be wise; keep your mind on the right course. Don't associate with those who drink too much wine or with those who gorge themselves on meat.
—Proverbs 23:19-20

READ: PROVERBS 23:19-21; PSALM 16:11

"Don't associate with those who drink too much wine or with those who gorge themselves on meat."

Why, you ask?

Because . . . "the drunkard and the glutton will become poor, and grogginess will clothe them in rags" (Proverbs 23:21).

Well, that is very important to know!

"But I'm not an adult!" you might say. "I definitely don't have to worry about drinking too much wine or eating too much steak." Actually, this proverb still relates to your life in many ways! Maybe your "too much" is sugar or dessert! Or maybe it's not too much food, but it's too much wasting time and not enough responsibility. There are all kinds of examples of how too much of a simple thing can turn in the wrong direction. And once you're turned in the wrong direction, the confusion can make it really difficult to come out with a good result. You might not reflect who you really are if you spend too much time in the fun zone instead of in the smart zone!

You've worked so hard to learn about wisdom and all that Solomon is teaching you about healthy choices, growing your smarts, and developing your relationship with God. You don't want to throw that away in an instant by lacking self-control. It's always good to slow down and think things through. Celebrating and relaxing is good, but so is knowing when to settle down. So the next time you're faced with the decision to stay up too late, eat too much sugar, or spend time with friends who might not bring out the best in you, take a minute to pause.

Even though you're young, these days are when you'll decide what you want to be and who you want to reflect!

Dear Lord,

You are the best party I can go to! You are with me everywhere I go, and You are full of celebration! Thank You for showing me the way to true joy and happiness through self-control. I love being with You and showing others who You are. Amen.

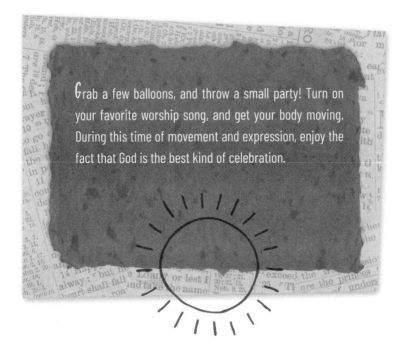

Grab a few balloons, and throw a small party! Turn on your favorite worship song, and get your body moving. During this time of movement and expression, enjoy the fact that God is the best kind of celebration.

85

YOUR PARENTS' JOY

Let your father and mother have joy, and let her who gave birth to you rejoice.—Proverbs 23:25

READ: PROVERBS 23:22-25

Until you are a parent, you will never understand the absolute joy *you* bring to *your* parents and those who take care of you. When they held you in their arms for the first time—and a million times since—you filled them with bursting pride, radiating love, and immense joy. All the words in this book could not convey to you the love and joy you bring to your parents. Truly.

You probably don't think a lot about how your daily decisions, especially those big life decisions, affect your parents. But just as they experience intense joy and pride just from being your parents, they also experience intense worry and regret over any poor decisions you make. As you get older, your decisions will have more and more ability to affect the rest of your life. And your parents know this. They've been there.

As a parent, Solomon knows this too. And while he talks about the joy you can bring to your mother and father, he also offers a warning, some advice: "Listen to your father" (Proverbs 23:22). "Buy—and do not sell—truth, wisdom, instruction, and understanding" (v. 23). Solomon knows that just as much as "the father of a righteous son will rejoice" (v. 24), the parents of an unrighteous child will mourn.

The proverbs in this book are not just words. They are wisdom, God-given wisdom, from the world's wisest king, recorded in writing for his own son. They are words that will guide you in a righteous life. It is guidance that when followed will bring you—and your parents—delight, joy, and rejoicing.

Dear God,
    Thank You for my parents and the other adults who love me. Forgive me for the times when I've disobeyed them, when I've brought them disappointment or sadness. Help me to seek and follow truth, wisdom, instruction, and understanding so that I may bring true and lasting joy to myself and those around me. Amen.

Read Proverbs 23:23. Now, let's make a price list. List some items like those Solomon mentions in this verse: "truth, wisdom, instruction, and understanding." Beside each item, imagine and list its worth. How valuable are these items? What would it cost to buy them? And why does Solomon say that we should not sell them? Consider this value of wisdom and understanding any time you receive them from your parents and teachers and those who are guiding you in your life.

86

GREEN WITH ENVY

Don't envy the evil or desire to be with them, for their hearts plan violence, and their words stir up trouble.
—Proverbs 24:1-2

READ: PROVERBS 24:1-4; PSALM 84:11

Have you ever heard the words "green with envy"? The phrase is believed to have come from the talented writer William Shakespeare, but our author, Solomon, wrote about envy long before old Will. Envy and jealousy are close companions, and their very presence can cause trouble to brew. Can you think of a time when you were unhappy with what you had simply because you saw and wanted what someone else had instead? That is envy!

Sometimes envy is about stuff—wanting the same cool shoes as Evan or wishing your family had a pool like Kara. Today's proverb talks about a different kind of envy: wanting to be around evil people and be what they are. Maybe you see how the school bully seems to get whatever he wants. Or how the girl who cheats on the tests has the best grades. You wonder if doing the wrong things with the wrong people might pay off.

But Solomon is warning us to stop envy in its tracks. All this envy can cause discontent to work its way into our hearts and lead us to bad choices. The next time you find yourself seeing what someone else has or does and then feeling sad or jealous inside, talk to God about it. Thank Him for your blessings because cultivating gratitude is a great way to fight envy, and being thankful works in the opposite direction of jealousy or discontent. God promises not to withhold any good thing from those who walk with Him well; you can rest in the fact that He already sees what you need (and He knows what you want too).

Dear Jesus,

Thank You for seeing my needs ahead of time. You know what I need, what I hope for, and what is good for me. I ask You to bring peace to my heart and keep me from envy and from evil. I want to be grateful and see the blessings that come from living a life focused on You. Amen.

Find a friend or family member and play a few games of tic-tac-toe! All those X's and O's can be a good reminder of the importance of wise choices. To win, you have to think ahead and watch for traps. If you don't pay attention, the other player can block you and keep you from your goal.

Have fun lining up your X's or O's while the other player does the same. After your game, think about how you can watch out for traps such as envy and discontent this week. Don't let envy block your focus on a life lived for God!

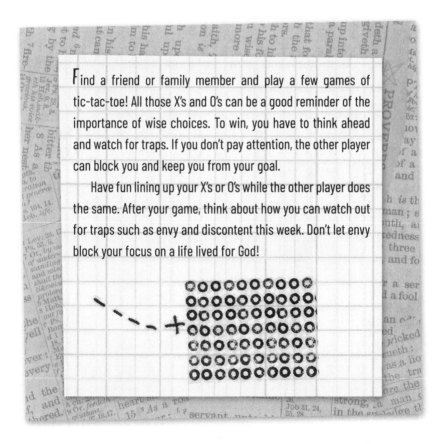

87

BRAINPOWER

A wise warrior is better than a strong one, and a man of knowledge than one of strength.—Proverbs 24:5

READ: PROVERBS 24:5–9

If you could choose any superpower, what would it be? X-ray vision? The ability to leap a tall building in a single bound? The ability to see the future?

Well, wise ol' Solomon has a secret superpower for us all: *wisdom*.

Okay, so maybe you saw that coming. (You have the ability to see the future!) But let's really think about it for a minute. "A wise warrior is better than a strong one." Is that true?

Let's ask David. You remember him, right? He was the youngest son of Jesse, out tending the sheep while his older brothers were at war. But when he went to visit his brothers, he found them and the rest of the Israelite army cowering in front of the giant, Goliath. David stepped up to that giant and said, "You come against me with a sword, spear, and javelin, but I come against you in the name of the LORD of Armies" (1 Samuel 17:45). Want to guess who won the battle that day?

And it turns out, this same David became Solomon's father. So when Solomon says, "A wise warrior is better than a strong one," he's not just giving you a fortune-cookie saying. He might be talking about his dad! He no doubt heard the firsthand accounts of how wisdom won the battle that day, not only for his father, but also for God's people.

So maybe before we start seeking far-fetched superpowers, we should start with the one right here in our hands: wisdom. Because it can win far more battles than mere superpowers ever could.

What would you look like as a superhero? Let's see it! You could draw a diagram of yourself in your suit with all your gadgets and powers. Or you could draw you in action, leaping a building in a single bound. Or maybe, just maybe, draw a picture of you using your super brainpower to bring down the evils of this world.

88

WISDOM = HOPE

Eat honey, my son, for it is good, and the honeycomb is sweet to your palate; realize that wisdom is the same for you. If you find it, you will have a future, and your hope will never fade.—Proverbs 24:13-14

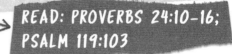

READ: PROVERBS 24:10-16; PSALM 119:103

Don't you love when you eat a treat that tastes delicious and is also healthy for you? Honey is one of those sweets! Did you know that raw honey can not only be used in dessert, but it can also heal wounds, soothe a sore throat, help a stomachache, and so much more? It's a powerhouse of health and sweetness all in one! In just one spoonful of raw honey, you get a good dose of antioxidants, you can cleanse your skin from bacteria, fight infections, and sweeten food naturally. It can help protect you from allergies, kill fungus (eeeewwwww!), and even make some really great candy!

Solomon says that something else is similar to honey. You guessed it, wisdom! He says eat it, learn about it, and enjoy its sweetness! It will fill your belly with good things like health, nourishment, protection, and healing—and it also "tastes" delicious! When wisdom is in your belly, you have hope and a future. You can look forward to all the ways God will lead you in your life and all the opportunities He will create so that you can learn and grow.

As you enjoy these sweet gifts, thank God for His blessings and for His Word. In Psalm 119, the Bible goes on to say: "How sweet your word is to my taste—sweeter than honey to my mouth" (v. 103). So in all things wise, healthy, and tasty—be glad!

SWEET!

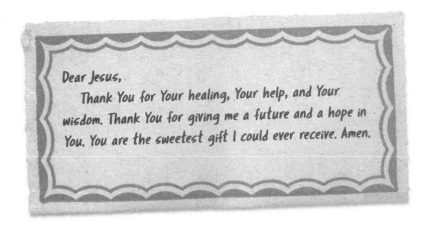

Dear Jesus,

Thank You for Your healing, Your help, and Your wisdom. Thank You for giving me a future and a hope in You. You are the sweetest gift I could ever receive. Amen.

Find five different snacks in your pantry that you can top with honey. You can look for tea, crackers, yogurt, or anything you think would taste good with a little sweetness on top. Which one is your favorite? Why? While you snack, reread today's Scripture and think again about the meaning of sweetness.

SOLOMON SAYS: *Go back to page 48 for more on our yummy topic: honey!*

89

KNOW WHO YOU ARE

Do not fret because of evildoers or be envious of the
wicked, for the evildoer has no future hope, and the lamp
of the wicked will be snuffed out.—Proverbs 24:19-20 NIV

READ: PROVERBS 24:17-29

Envy seems to have reached a new height in this century. What started with magazines showing us perfect humans and perfect homes has morphed into social media showing us the perfectly staged lives of everyone we know.

Of course, we've since learned that "perfect humans" are altered photos and "perfect homes" are staged. Ads showcasing the latest fashion and the next great tech toy only exist to make us buy more things. We all know this. And still, we seem to be always comparing, always wanting what someone else has.

The Bible has a word for this: *coveting*. More specifically, "Do not covet your neighbor's house . . . or anything that belongs to your neighbor" (Exodus 20:17). It's one of the Ten Commandments, the Big Ten, the top ten rules God wants us to follow.

Solomon gets a little more specific in today's proverb. He tells us not to envy the wicked, which seems like common sense, and yet . . . When you see someone doing something wrong and getting away with it, don't you just wish that maybe you could do that too? But Solomon is quick to remind us where that kind of behavior leads. And it is certainly a future *not* to be envied.

Know who you are and who created you (Ephesians 2:10). Know how uniquely and wonderfully you are made (Psalm 139:14). And know your purpose (Matthew 28:19). Knowing these things will protect you from envy, will keep you from coveting, and will keep you on the path God created just for you.

Dear God,

    Thank You for creating me uniquely and wonderfully. Protect me from envy, from wanting what others have, from wanting to do what they do. Help me to know Your unique gifts and purposes for me, and help me to focus on them so that I can do what You created me to do. Amen.

Make a list of all the unique and wonderful things about you—*yes, you.* Think of all the gifts God has given you, the things you have learned, and the things you can do. When you're finished with the list, go and do one of those things that God has uniquely gifted you to do. Remember your list anytime you start to compare yourself with others, and remind yourself that God has uniquely gifted you too!

SLACKERS NEVER REAP

I went by the field of a slacker and by the vineyard of one lacking sense. Thistles had come up everywhere, weeds covered the ground, and the stone wall was ruined.
—Proverbs 24:30-31

READ: PROVERBS 24:30-34

Have you ever been in a cluttered, unorganized room and felt anxious because of it? When a space is chaotic and hasn't been cared for, cleaning it can seem like a ton of work. But it's really hard to enjoy the good things in your day when you know there's messy work to do.

Perhaps that's what Solomon was experiencing when he described the field of a slacker and the vineyard of a fool (a person without sense). Solomon described these places as having all kinds of thorns and weeds springing up with a broken wall around it. That sounds like such a sad sight, doesn't it?

A field that was supposed to produce such wonderful fruit ended up being something that was left abandoned. Instead of being pruned and receiving regular care, it grew weeds and prickly plants. It wasn't able to be successful or even enjoyed; instead, it was left to be ugly.

Aren't you glad that God doesn't leave us to be that way? Unlike this field's owner, God is no slacker, and He makes perfect sense. Sometimes it might feel difficult to do all the things God asks of us. Maybe you're tired, or maybe you just don't want to follow the rules, but God is persistent with us. He reminds us to return to Him and follow Him so that we produce fruit and grow into people who are caring, kind, and helpful!

So, the next time you don't feel like picking up your room, spending time studying the Bible, or listening to your parents, just remember: weeds will grow in an abandoned place! But if you have compassion on yourself and do your work, your surroundings and your life and faith will show fruit.

Dear Lord,

You are so persistent in Your care of me! Help me to remember that You discipline and take care of the ones You love. When I am disciplined and do not slack, I will receive a full reward in You. Thank You for teaching me a bigger way to live! Amen.

Go to your room, and set a timer for ten minutes. See how fast you can clean up, organize, dust, vacuum, or make your bed! Every day, try a ten-minute cleanup and see how it feels. Your room will undoubtedly be more fresh and welcoming. Now think about what happens when you work hard to keep your heart clean and uncluttered. It will be a welcome place for faith to grow!

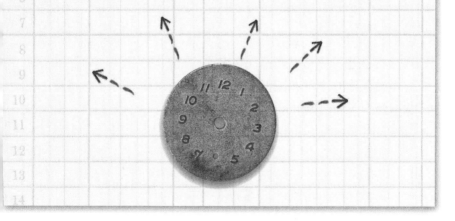

SOLOMON SAYS: Go back to page 32 for a reminder on how God organizes the world.

SEEK AND FIND

It is God's privilege to conceal things and the king's privilege to discover them.—Proverbs 25:2 NLT

READ: PROVERBS 25:1-10

Imagine for a minute all the things that God must know. What the world looked like before the first human set foot on it . . . What Mars smells like . . . What a worm is thinking . . . And deeper than just factoids, He knows the answers to our deepest questions, like why we're here and what *exactly* happens when we die.

Any question you could ever think of, God already knows the answer to it.

Job pondered this same topic, asking, "Where then does wisdom come from?" (Job 28:20 NIV). He explained that we can search the depths of the sea and never find it. We can try to buy it with precious jewels and gold. But true wisdom, real answers, "God understands the way to it and he alone knows where it dwells, for he views the ends of the earth and sees everything under the heavens" (Job 28:23-24 NIV).

What God knows—and what we don't—is infinite. And so begins a lifetime of seek and find, with God holding all the answers in His hand, and us, His children, forever seeking Him and the answers He holds.

Whatever you're searching for, whatever you need, God has an abundance of it. Whatever you've lost, whatever you're missing, He knows where to find it. And whatever your question, whatever your problem, He holds the solution.

As you go through life, you will no doubt have needs and problems, questions and mysteries that arise. But as God's children, you will never have to go far to find everything you need.

Dear God,

Your wisdom and knowledge are infinite. I know this. I do. Help me to remember this when I get frustrated or when I try to find answers elsewhere. Help me to remember that I can find all the answers by seeking You. Amen.

Set a timer for five minutes. During that time, write down every question you can think of. Questions about anything: trout fishing, the purpose of life, quantum physics, whatever. Don't edit yourself. Just write down whatever questions come to mind. When you're finished, review your list and talk to God about whatever questions you need answers to.

BE AN ENCOURAGER!

A word spoken at the right time is like gold apples in silver settings. A wise correction to a receptive ear is like a gold ring or an ornament of gold.—Proverbs 25:11-12

READ: PROVERBS 25:11-28

Have you ever had a friend come alongside you when you're struggling and say just the right thing to lift you up? It's almost like they know just what to do to make you feel better or make you smile. Their words can feel so refreshing and turn your whole day around.

Proverbs shares some important advice on the topic of encouragement—and also correction. Solomon records that a word spoken at the right time is the perfect fit to someone who needs it, and correcting someone who is willing to learn is just as beautiful! Sometimes we can get caught up in trying to fix everyone or everything around us. Sad, but true.

At times, people just don't know when to quit, or sometimes they just don't know when to be quiet. And that can be hurtful. But when the right person comes along, who is kind and gentle, and who speaks the truth with love inside, it can change everything. And when someone who wants to learn and grow (and is willing to be corrected) listens, that can also change everything!

So, in all things big and small, seek to be the kind of person who knows when to encourage others! And when someone wise is offering you gentle correction, open your ears wide enough to hear what that person is truly saying. Encouraging someone at the right time or being encouraged to be wise is always beautiful and valuable. It's just like striking gold!

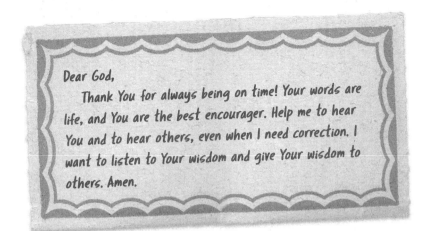

Dear God,

Thank You for always being on time! Your words are life, and You are the best encourager. Help me to hear You and to hear others, even when I need correction. I want to listen to Your wisdom and give Your wisdom to others. Amen.

Let's play telephone! Grab a few family members or friends, and sit in a line. The first person in line makes up an encouraging sentence and then quietly tells that sentence to the next person in line. Each person will then whisper the sentence to the next person until the final person exclaims the sentence out loud.

Was the sentence the same or different than the original? Take the opportunity to enjoy a good laugh, and be reminded that encouraging words can sometimes get muddled over time. Although this game isn't exactly like direct encouragement, it is a good reminder to speak to each other clearly and to have a sense of humor in the process (even if the words don't always come out right)!

93

BEWARE OF FOOLS AND FLATTERY

As a dog returns to its vomit, so also a fool repeats his foolishness. . . . A lying tongue hates those it crushes, and a flattering mouth causes ruin.—Proverbs 26:11, 28

--→ READ: PROVERBS 26

Jesus often told parables to explain things. He would use objects and situations familiar to the people and the time period He spoke to. Gardening and grapes, bread and birds were all objects and situations that He used to convey messages about the kingdom and character of God.

Throughout Proverbs, and especially in Proverbs 26, Solomon takes a similar approach. But Solomon's approach is a little less, eh, *refined*. He uses dog vomit and madmen and flaming darts and crushing stones to convey his points. But his messages are no less memorable.

Have you ever seen someone make the same mistake over and over and over again? Imagine how God must feel when He sees us returning to the things we *know* that we shouldn't be doing. When He has given us delicious gifts to enjoy, we keep returning to, well, you know. *Yuck.*

Do you know someone who is always being dishonest? And then maybe says something like, "I was only joking!" To God (and the rest of us), he looks "like a madman who throws flaming darts and deadly arrows" (Proverbs 26:18-19). It's a pretty accurate description, right?

And the person who's always scheming, who always has something up her sleeve? When we're tempted to do the same, it helps to recall the image Solomon gives us in Proverbs 26:27: "The one who digs a pit will fall into it, and whoever rolls a stone—it will come back on him." I'd rather just avoid the stone and the pit altogether, thank you very much.

Although the images Solomon uses may be jolting, he wants to make sure that you walk away with a message, with wisdom you won't soon forget. And if it takes dog vomit to keep us from living a life of foolishness, well, I guess I'm okay with that.

Dear God,

Thank You for wise king Solomon who chose to share his wisdom with us. Help me to do whatever it takes to remember these messages and apply them to my life. Help me to avoid the pit and the crushing stone and never to return to my own yuck. Amen.

How about you write your own message using imagery? You can either use words or a drawing—or both—to illustrate it. First, take a minute to think back on the wisdom we've learned from Solomon. Using objects and situations that people of *your* time period will appreciate and understand, create a message of wisdom with them. When you're finished writing or drawing your message, go and actually share it with someone you know. As you do, you're following in the footsteps of the best, wisest storytellers this world has ever known.

94

BOASTING RARELY WORKS

Don't boast about tomorrow, for you don't know what a day might bring. Let another praise you, and not your own mouth—a stranger, and not your own lips.
—Proverbs 27:1–2

READ: PROVERBS 27:1–13

Bragging never looks good. Have you ever noticed that? More often than not, when a person starts bragging, it's actually the beginning of their defeat. What they accomplished in order to start boasting in the first place loses its value, and it gets lost in the bad behavior of their loud cheering.

When you win at something, what do you typically do? Do you go around telling everyone the awesome thing you did and shout it from the rooftops? Or do you share your success in a way that is honoring and gentle? It can make a world of difference.

Proverbs 27:2 gives some good advice: "Let another praise you, and not your own mouth—a stranger, and not your own lips." When someone else brags about you or praises you for what you've accomplished, you know that God sees you for what you've done and that others do as well. It's a sign of faith to let others celebrate your good works instead of trying to call attention to yourself.

To read more about boasting and humility, see 1 Peter 5:6, which reminds readers to "Humble yourselves, therefore, under the mighty hand of God, so that he may exalt you at the proper time." When life is all said and done, you'll be loved and remembered more for what others say about you than what you say about yourself. Even when you win at something big, allow the time and space in your heart to celebrate with God. He is with you in the journey and in the celebration. When you choose to boast about God instead, others will naturally come alongside you to celebrate!

Dear God,

I want to be a good sport. Help me to celebrate my successes deeply with You! Give me the self-control to know when to share and when to allow others to honor me. Winning isn't really winning if boasting is a result. Please give me the grace to stay humble at all times. Amen.

Look at every person in your family, and write down one way that each of them is winning at life! Make sure to tell them what you noted and encourage them for all the hard work they have done in that area of life. Celebrate their successes with them, and affirm that you see and love them!

FOCUS ON RELATIONSHIP

Iron sharpens iron, and one person sharpens another.
—Proverbs 27:17

READ: PROVERBS 27:14–27

If you're not a blacksmith (an old-school, fire-forged metal worker), the phrase "iron sharpens iron" may not immediately conjure up vivid images for you. So let's think about it for a minute, because the image and the message Solomon is trying to convey is a powerful one.

We all know what iron is, right? Have you ever held it in your hand? Maybe a wrought-iron stair railing? Or a heavy metal fire poker by the fireplace? Technically, it may be steel, but the effect is the same. Back in Solomon's day, iron was a really hard, heavy metal.

And we can all readily understand how not everything could sharpen iron, right? Wood, for instance, is softer than iron. If scraped against a block of iron, it would only shave and splinter away. It wouldn't sharpen the iron. It would take a hard metal, a metal at least as strong as iron to sharpen iron itself.

That's where we come in. That's why it is so important that we gain wisdom, that we strengthen ourselves in the faith. The people around us are going to need to be strengthened. They're going to need to be sharpened. And just like it takes iron to sharpen iron, it takes a faith-filled person to sharpen another person.

For this reason, too, it matters what kind of people you hang around. Are you hanging around people who are going to sharpen you? Or are you hanging around people who are going to make you rust and ruin?

Iron sharpens iron. And by continually learning and growing stronger in our faith, we not only strengthen ourselves, but we also sharpen those around us, strengthening the entire kingdom of God.

Dear God,

Thank You for putting strong people of faith around me. Thank You for all the ways that they've strengthened and sharpened me. Help me to continue to seek You, to continue to seek Your wisdom, and to continue to grow stronger in my faith so that I may help to strengthen and sharpen the people around me. Amen.

Think about some of the people in your life who sharpen you. What could you do today, right now, to help sharpen someone else? You could send them a card or a Bible verse. You could invite them to church or just go ride bikes with them. Do one thing today that will help to build up and sharpen another person. And continue to look for—and *act on*—those opportunities every day.

96

HONESTY RECEIVES MERCY

The one who conceals his sins will not prosper, but whoever confesses and renounces them will find mercy.
—Proverbs 28:13

READ: PROVERBS 28:1-28

Have you ever noticed when you try to hide your mistakes that it can actually make everything worse? Doing something wrong can make you feel bad enough, and then hiding the mess-up is just a recipe for disaster. That's because hiding sin keeps your mistake, your feelings, and even your heart *in the dark*. There they churn in the shadows, making everything else a bit toxic so that nothing can heal. But if you confess your sin to God and admit that you were wrong, you can step out of the dark and receive God's forgiveness.

You can also give your struggles some light with a trusted friend, teacher, or family member. When you tell someone about what is going on, where you made a mistake, or where you just can't seem to get unstuck, a listening ear can be the grace you need to grow. It might even keep you from sickness, guilt, or worry! That is God's mercy to us.

Confession can feel a bit embarrassing at first, and you might feel ashamed, but just remember that all humans have sins and struggles! When you confess your sins and turn away from them, you know that God will always meet you. He promises us that. Allowing Jesus into our darkness gives us the ability to receive His truth and His grace. Being honest about where we struggle is a good way to keep the light on in our lives.

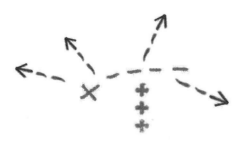

Dear Jesus,

Give me humility and courage to confess my sins. Thank You for grace and mercy in return. I submit my mistakes, my struggles, and my heart to You. Help me live in the light so that darkness cannot dwell in me. Please give me Your mercy so that I can give mercy to others. Amen.

Ever heard the song "This Little Light of Mine"? It's an oldie but a goodie. If you know the words, revisit that little kid inside you by saying or singing them out loud as a declaration of who you are in Jesus. We are all God's children, no matter what age we are. We can let our light shine on others and also let His light shine within us and uncover our hidden struggles. If you don't know the words to the song, look them up or ask a friend. Take the time to read them aloud or sing them for the first time. Then shine that light!

SOLOMON SAYS: Go to page 134 to read more on mercy.

97

WISDOM WINS

An evil person is caught by sin, but the righteous one sings and rejoices.—Proverbs 29:6

READ: PROVERBS 29:1–27

We're nearing the end of our study with Solomon—at least as far as this book goes. And Proverbs 29 seems to be a bit of a lightning round on some of the things we've learned.

In this chapter alone, we see "the righteous flourish, the people rejoice" (v. 2), a wise man bringing joy to his father (v. 3), a just king who brings stability (v. 4), the wise turning away anger (v. 8), a fair judge (v. 14), a child who brings peace of mind (v. 17), an honored humble spirit (v. 23), and a protected one who trusts in the Lord (v. 25).

But we also see the stiff-necked (v. 1) and the wicked (v. 2). We see the destruction of wealth (v. 3) and an evil person caught by sin (v. 6). We see the mockers (v. 8) and the bloodthirsty (v. 10), the angry (v. 11) and the liars (v. 12). We see the arrogant (v. 21) and the hot-tempered (v. 22), the unjust and detestable (v. 27).

The bottom line is this: there's a competition, a fight, a war between wise and foolish, good and evil out there. And spoiler alert: wisdom wins. The good, righteous, wise, God-seeking side, without a doubt, wins in the end.

If this whole study has taught us anything, hasn't it taught us which one we want to be, which group we want to be in, which side of the fight we want to be on? Sure, in the end, wisdom wins. But in the meantime, it also creates a life worth living.

Dear God,
Thank You for teaching wisdom to Your people. Help me to choose every day to seek wisdom and to be an example of wisdom for others. Help me every day to choose a life worth living, a life that serves and honors You. Amen.

Set a timer for two minutes. During that time, see how many important lessons, phrases, or descriptive words you can remember from this study of Proverbs. When you're finished, take the time to read over your list and add to it however you want. Let it represent what you've learned so far in your study of wisdom, reminding you of who you want to be and maybe even who you don't.

JUST ENOUGH

Two things I ask of you; don't deny them to me before I die: Keep falsehood and deceitful words far from me. Give me neither poverty nor wealth; feed me with the food I need.
—Proverbs 30:7-8

READ: PROVERBS 30:1-33

"Feed me with the food I need."

That is one of the wisest statements we have discussed up to this point with good old Solomon!

Ever notice that when you eat a bit too much, it doesn't feel good? And ever notice that when you don't have enough, it is equally distracting? It's as if God knows (of course He does!) that what we need is right in the middle of hunger and gluttony. He knows what is necessary and what is not. This is the evidence that God is a good Dad! He goes before us to prepare what He knows is important for us to grow and learn, and He also protects us from receiving things that could hurt us or confuse us.

When we stay in that middle place of full reliance on God, we really do learn how to pray and be with Him. First Thessalonians 5:16-18 reminds us to "Rejoice always, pray constantly, give thanks in everything; for this is God's will for you in Christ Jesus." That is, in fact, the best way to keep away anything false and deceitful, as well as too much or too little in life. It is right in the middle of the heart of God Himself. And that is the most wise, smart, safe, and loving place to be.

ENOUGH

Dear God,

Being with You is the best! I am so grateful that Your way is perfect. You give me safety, peace, and exactly what I need in every circumstance. Help me to rejoice, pray, and always give thanks. Amen.

One of the best ways to balance yourself in a world full of wants and needs is to enjoy what God has created. Take a walk in nature today, and soak up the sunshine on your face. When we enjoy the simplicity and beauty of God's life around us and His movement in us, we find that we have everything we need.

99

SPEAK UP!

"Speak up for those who cannot speak for themselves. Defend the rights of all those who have nothing. Speak up and judge fairly. Defend the rights of the poor and needy."
—Proverbs 31:8-9 ICB

READ: PROVERBS 31:1-9

So what are you going to do with all this wisdom you've learned? Are you going to keep it all to yourself? Are you going to use it only in your own life?

No. No, you are not.

You're going to use it to speak up and speak into other people's lives! You're going to "speak up for those who cannot speak for themselves" and "defend the rights of all those who have nothing" (Proverbs 31:8 ICB). You're going to "defend the rights of the poor and needy" (v. 9).

Why? Because that's what the wise and righteous do. Because there are people out there whose parents don't buy them books about wisdom. There are people with no access to the Word of God. There are people who are so focused on finding immediate needs like food or clothing or safety that they lack the capacity to widen their search for anything as wonderful as wisdom.

And that's where you come in. Take this wisdom that you've been fortunate enough to gain, and spread it around. Look out at the world around you through the enlightened lens of wisdom, and see where there is injustice and wickedness and foolishness. And *speak up.*

That is the beauty and burden of wisdom. Now that you have it, you must use it not only for the benefit of yourself but also for the benefit of all.

○○ ○○○ ○○○ ○○○ ○○○

Dear God,

Thank You for this wonderful discovery of wisdom. Please help me to use it to see others as You see them. Help me to know the needs of the voiceless and to speak up for them in wisdom. Help this to be a never-ending desire and purpose of my life, to speak up for those who can't speak up for themselves. Amen.

Look around for those who need you to speak up for them. You may already have some people in mind, but take it a step further. Talk to your parents or leaders at your church about how you can be a voice for those who are voiceless or defenseless or needy. Could you organize a book drive for a shelter? Could you collect food for a family in need? Is there a neighbor or classmate who just needs a friend? Create a plan and use your wisdom and your voice to speak up for those who cannot speak up for themselves.

100

A JOURNEY IN WISDOM

Strength and honor are her clothing, and she can laugh at the time to come. Her mouth speaks wisdom, and loving instruction is on her tongue.—Proverbs 31:25–26

READ: PROVERBS 31:10–31

You want to know what is really fun? *Laughing!* Doesn't it feel so amazing to laugh? It takes away stress, it fills us with goodness, and it makes our day bright. Every day is a good day to laugh.

And since we are at the end of this journey in Proverbs, today's Scripture is the perfect place to finish. In the final chapter of the text, the Proverbs 31 woman is described. And even if you're not a girl, the description of this woman can be used to encourage and strengthen anyone. She is a person of wisdom, courage, instruction, and smarts! She follows God closely, so she is able to lead and help others.

The Proverbs 31 woman has so much faith that she laughs, yes laughs, at the future! If she is laughing at the future, then she is full of God's love, joy, peace, and power. Who doesn't want to live with that kind of confidence and boldness? She is the perfect example of all that Solomon has been teaching throughout the last one hundred days. As you finish reading this book, be reminded of all you can gain from following the advice you've received. You have come so far! You should be so proud of yourself and all that you've learned.

To close out your time with Solomon, take a few minutes to celebrate, thank God, and pray about your future. When following these wise words and the example of this woman in Proverbs 31, you are sure to have some very bright days ahead of you!

Dear God,

Thank You for this journey in wisdom and all You have taught me. I am so grateful for the opportunity to learn, grow, and read these pages. Thank You for blessing Solomon and for giving me instructions for life so that I can love my journey and love those around me. Amen.

Take a few minutes to look back at all the pages you've read. See how far you've journeyed over these last few months!

Can you pick out two or three devotions that were your favorite? Why did you like them, and what did they mean to you? Be sure to share them with others, and tell them more about what you've learned. You are awesome, wise, and amazing—congratulations!

Sarah Humphrey is a wife and homeschool mom to three kids while also working as an artist, author, and voice actor. Her writing and doodling can be found in her devotional, *40 Days to a Joyful Motherhood*, and her voice in several commercials, children's books, and audiobooks. She loves encouraging women and kids to embrace self-care, utilize their gifts, and become leaders in the community around them.

Amy Parker has written more than seventy books for children, teens, and adults, with over 2 million copies sold. She has collaborated with authors ranging from *New York Times* bestsellers to her very own son. Two of these collaborations—*Firebird* and *Courageous Teens*—are recipients of *Christian Retailing's* Best Awards. But Amy's greatest reward is being a wife to Daniel and a mom to their amazing sons, Michael and Ethan.